Deep Tracks
to Follow

Deep Tracks
to Follow

Gene R. Stark

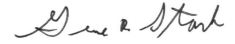

NORTH STAR PRESS OF ST. CLOUD, INC.
St. Cloud, Minnesota

Previous works:

Flyover Seasons (2011)
Tracks in the Mud (2012)
Water and Dirt (2013)

For more information, please visit:
www.flyovercountryscribe.com

Copyright © 2014 Gene Stark

ISBN: 978-0-87839-767-9

First edition: May 2014

Printed in the United States of America

Published by
North Star Press of St. Cloud, Inc.
P.O. Box 451
St. Cloud, MN 56302

T he month of February in Minnesota is a cruel month. Only by God's grace and the luck of the calendar-makers has it at least turned out to be the shortest month in actual days. Perhaps the greatest claim to fame for the month of February in Minnesota is its great value as a month to make four-wheel-drive vehicle commercials or for testing heavy duty car batteries.

It was one of those mornings, after a snowfall, that I remember the snow lay deep before me, the wind twisted wisps of snow into my tracks, and the cold, warmth-deprived sun laid shadows across the yard. There is rarely a snowfall so large or severe in Minnesota that it warrants a title or some historical remembrance. The so-called Armistice Day Blizzard comes to mind and the great snowstorm that struck on Halloween, in more recent memory, but the day I recall in February of 1999 had no title and has no historical remembrance. I recall only the tracks I left behind me as I walked out to my office from our house.

I've been most blessed, in that my commute to work during most of my years has been only a short walk from the house out to my office which is connected to our greenhouse operation. No slippery, white-knuckle drives among half-asleep, winter-crazed, early-morning drivers.

It's still the tracks I remember on that cold, snowy day and it's the memory of looking behind me and watching my little Labrador retriever pup following me. He scratched and climbed from each cavernous impression in the snow, to the next one, disappearing for an instant in each of my step-marks, only to reappear and struggle to the next track. The little rusty-yellow pup, frost crystals glistening on his perky little whiskers, followed me that day, the sun causing the snow to sparkle and contrast upon his off-white little face.

The brown eyes, ever intent upon me seemed to exude determination and boundless energy. February was a tough time to be a pup—a little fur-ball, less than half knee-high. But those brown eyes were ever-intent upon me. There was a depth of knowing in those piercing little dark eyes, with their humbling look of awe, a look I don't think I deserved.

Timing is everything, and I suppose that is especially true as we contemplate taking upon ourselves the raising of a puppy. We had dogs in the household, because our son and our youngest daughter had committed to having dogs, and had followed through with taking care of their dogs. I had no responsibility with those dogs, other than the not-so-small commitment of buying the food.

Now, I had to decide if I was ready again for a dog. Business and family had become a bit less demanding as children grew up and things stabilized and blossomed on the business-front. I felt I could spend the time, do justice to a dog, and enjoy the commitment. The other compelling reason for the dog was the timing and the availability. A friend had spoken of his exceptional male black Lab and his son's tremendous female yellow Lab. Both dogs were extraordinary and exceptional hunting partners. The most important part of the scenario was the fact that the pair had reared a litter of pups. They were born in January and that meant the young dogs would be nearly grown by fall and would be able to begin hunting in the next upland and waterfowl season.

"Let's take a look at them," I suggested to my wife. I knew Muriel to be an even greater sucker for puppies than myself. My youngest daughter, another true dog-lover at heart, was also not to be left out of the decision. In fact Jenessa and I made the final pick, knowing that any little bundle of fur, either black or yellow, would totally capture the heart of Mom.

The ever-changing mass of black and yellow scampered before us. There were six black pups and six yellow ones. It was a mind-boggling selection. Should it be a male or a female? Should it be a male black or a female yellow? Of course it was obvious that the possible combinations of choices were extensive.

While we watched those pups, we observed the mother, whose name was Kelsae, and the father, Beau. Both parents seemed pretty easy-going, allowing us to handle the little offspring, to play with them, and observe. The pups were obviously being well socialized and the parents were used to people.

The Labrador retriever, being one of the most popular of all dogs, has come upon the popularity honestly. They are people-lovers, bred over the ages to work closely with their human counterparts. They're team-players, who realize even in hunting situations they have the nose and instinct their human companion lacks, but if they want to retrieve during the outing, they must cooperate. Indeed the retriever-portion of a Labrador's instinct, is the lion's-share of its heart. They live to return things to their human friends. Perhaps that is also the reason they are such good companion-dogs for people with special needs. For me there was no decision to be made as to which breed I wanted. Having had Labradors before, I was fully aware of their strengths and, of course, their weaknesses as well.

All of these thoughts did little to help settle upon an individual. Again, the theories are endless. Does one pick a puppy that is least aggressive, therefore compliant and easily trainable? Should the pup be a middle-of-the-pack individual—a signal which might indicate the best of all dispositions? Maybe the first one out of the door signifies a puppy that will excel at all it attempts.

3

We observed and discussed all the ideas about picking a pup. I had been followed, as a youngster, by a black dog which became a mainstay in my early life. I had raised a yellow lab during my adolescence and that may have given me a bias towards the yellow lab.

Finally we made the enormous decision to go with a yellow pup. That cut the field in half. Six little roly-poly bundles of yellow fur now occupied our observation. Male or female? Muriel, of course saw the potential for some puppies with a female dog. She, as previously stated, is a big-time sucker for pups. I, maybe a bit more practical in this matter, figured more pups was a bit much. Of course neutering was another issue we would have to grapple with at a later time.

Having had mostly male dogs, I won out on the gender issue and we decided to go with a male. Now we had to get down to the final decision. That decision fell mostly to Jenessa and me. We probably wear our hearts on our sleeves to a great degree, more than others in our family, and now the final gut-feeling part of the decision was upon us.

When the food was put out, the pup that left the barn first caught my attention. The fact that he came out first wasn't so important, but he didn't go directly to the food, he had other interests. He stopped at every twig and every change in the dirt and grass patterns to sniff and investigate. His attention was totally drawn by a sparrow flying by. This pup had interests and potential far beyond eating. His color was that of a prairie sunset the night before a storm. I knew he would be trouble because he wanted to lead and would have a hard time allowing anyone to make up his mind for him. Yet there was a depth of expression in those eyes that told me he would know more than some of his litter-mates. Of course, the little fellow followed me as I walked and seemed to know there was a free lunch ticket to be gained by such activity. Yes, it happened to me again. Another one had gotten its claws into me. I was set up for another fall.

So we focused on him as we talked.

"Dad, how can you know what's in his heart?" my daughter asked.

"Only when I look into his eyes can I know."

"But how do you know?"

"I ignore his softness, his cute little nose, and the way his ears perk up when we talk. I only see into his eyes."

"What do you see in those eyes?"

"It's more what I don't see than what I do."

"What don't you see in this one?" she picked up the pup and handed the wiggling little fur-ball to me.

"I don't see single-mindedness. There's more on his mind than the bowl of puppy-chow on the ground. There's more than a dim, following stare."

"Can I look?"

"See that this one has a sparkle, a glimmer of more than just compliance. He'll be hard to train, but he'll learn to think. He has a spirit that will bond with ours."

"How do you know?"

"Already he watches my every move. We'll communicate by signals no one else will understand. He'll come to us like the first wolf that entered the cave of Man. We'll bring joy to each other and he will bring us pain."

"What do you mean, Dad?"

"Over time you'll know. Now put your ear to his chest and hear the joy of a heartbeat."

What started as a very analytical, practical decision came down to one of emotion, one of feeling and connection to things harder to analyze. Finally, it was the eyes, the bit of insight into the heart of the dog afforded by those brown little orbs. There was a depth in the way he looked at us, a promise of sagacity beyond that of his siblings. The way he cocked his head when we held him, the utter confidence he exhibited when he snuggled deep into our arms and our hearts, snagged us. Oh, he hooked us badly there's no doubt. With those deep-brown eyes he put a collar around our necks, as surely as we put that blue band of leather on him just days later. We felt he wanted us. Yes, he picked us just as certainly as we responded.

The day he came home with us, shivering a bit as he sat on Jenessa's lap, he must have been wondering about the new step he was taking. We too, wondered what joys, what trials, what sorrows he would place upon us.

The naming, among a family of seven, did not come easily. Finally, I threw out the name "Roy." I had once had a yellow lab named Roy, a name probably appropriated from my Dad's love for the singing cowboy, Roy Rogers. By some miracle, all of our kids liked the name and "Roy" stuck.

Although Roy's mother was a registered Labrador retriever, coming from proven bloodlines, his father Beau was a talented stray who had shown up on the owner's doorstep one day. It was sort of a marriage of royalty and commoner that begat the dog named Roy and indeed he seemed to live up to both sides of the family. The tiny paws that would follow me during the first year, would grow to a full-sized set of dog feet which I would in turn follow across many fields and wetlands.

Twelve years later, as I pondered Roy's final day with me, I was struck by that snowy first February when he followed my tracks, never taking those bright, all-knowing eyes from me. On that last day with me, he still followed, on faltering and shaking legs, the eyes still brown, yet vacuous and searching, only sensing an image of me, as failing eyesight allowed.

I suppose I wasn't too hard to convince on the issue of where the puppy would live.

"We can't put such a little puppy outside in this kind of weather," Muriel stated unequivocally.

My only argument might have been that I had never raised a pup indoors before.

"We always had dogs in the house when I was growing up," she stated, and then named off a litany of house-raised dogs, not the least of which was named Frisky, who ironically seemed to have brought forth a goodly number of pups of her own.

We had a kennel outside and our youngest daughter had kept her dog outside, yet Roy was about to become my first indoor dog. We decided to acclimate him to a kennel box and of course the house-breaking process needed to begin immediately.

Muriel initially protested the kennel box. "You can't keep him in such a small space." Yet I think she finally believed Jenessa and me as we demonstrated that dogs have a need for a secure space, much as wild canines utilize dens. The pack mentality also began to become more evident to me as we kept a dog in our house. I, my wife, and my two youngest daughters Jolene and Jenessa became the immediate pack-mates, since we were the ones still most at home at the time. Of course such a little pup knew his place in the pecking order of the pack, so the training began. As Roy grew older he seemed to have aspirations of rising in the pack caste system and just who trained whom, I still wonder about quite a bit.

I feel that only when you raise a dog in the house can you really begin to understand the canine mentality. The issues of seniority in the pack and dominance issues really become clear when a dog is in the house. There is also much to be learned about dog training, when keeping a dog inside as opposed to keeping a dog outside. I truly believe a dog's potential is greatly enhanced by being around people at all times. The dog's vocabulary is much larger when he is exposed to constant talk. Dogs really are good observers and they learn much while just lying on the living room floor. In later years, as Roy reached his prime, I felt at times his vocabulary was much larger than that of a lot people I ran into.

Of course little Roy missed all his warm, furry littermates, and vocally expressed his displeasure at their absence the first night. I suppose Roy felt we should adopt the whole litter. He had known nothing other than the warmth and proximity of the litter and his mother.

"We have to leave him in his box," I argued, "it's the only way he'll get used to being alone. Besides, it is very important in the house-breaking process." There are two things my wife is compelled by nature to pick up: crying babies and whimpering pups. Of course Roy immediately stopped whimpering when Muriel picked him up. He soon taught Muriel to pick him up on command, the command being a heart-wrenching whine.

The first few nights the puppy would only sleep while curled up upon my wife as she slept on the couch. At first I could only protest and shake my head, yet all seemed calm and we all rested well. So much for the book, regarding puppy training.

I can still picture the furry little guy sprawled out upon my wife. The pup would spastically emit little jerks and twitches as he dreamed puppy-dreams of his warm mother and soft siblings. Perhaps there were dreams of times to come, of growing up and independence. For now he took the

Mutual contentment.

warmth and care, learning to become a human, from some one so good at it.

Now was indeed the formative time for our puppy. Soon his little paws tracked across our house as he confidently adjusted to his new home. He followed us and found interest in everything he encountered. The sound of his little tracks became music to our ears. House-breaking became the obsession of those early days. We were to keep him in his kennel-box and immediately upon getting him out, take him outside while saying, "Potty, potty." Of course he was often ready to go at that point, and responded pretty well. We learned to watch him like a hawk when he was in the house for any indication he needed to go out and do his business. Of course much of his training hinged upon our training and perception. Success and failure in the potty-training process abounded on a daily basis. Finally he seemed to get the concept of peeing and pooping outside. Fortunately dogs seem to be pretty meticulous about keeping clean, refusing to mess their kennel boxes, and eventually the transfer broadens to not messing up the house either.

Roy was a pretty dominant dog. Even as a pup he was ready to move up on the ladder of dominance. His challenges came on a daily basis. It was almost spring of that first year. There were patches of grass and mud showing through the snow, giving the little dog nice places to do his potty business outside the front door. He knew to go to the door when he needed to go to the bathroom. We were all trained to watch for any indication that he needed to go out. I remember the day, probably in March, when he went to the door and my son let him out.

"Go potty, Roy," my son said as he let the dog out the door. Roy stood there and just looked back, then came back to the door. My son let him back in and just as the little dog got into the entryway of the house, decided to go potty. I took it as a challenge—perhaps he felt he should move his potty area into the entryway of the house. That would be a very convenient place to go to the bathroom, especially on the blustery and cold days that are so prevalent in Minnesota. He challenged the wrong person on that issue. My son picked him up by the scruff of his neck with a good shake and a loud "No" and threw him outside again. After that Roy was golden about house-breaking and never had another "accident."

Scruff-shakes seemed to work miracles on that dog. I suspect he got plenty of them from his mother before he came home with us. Many instances of disobedience required a solid "No" and a scruff-shake. It only took once to teach him not to potty in the greenhouse. I truly believe that even when Roy weighed close to ninety pounds he still believed I could pick him up by the scruff of the neck and give him a shake. I became won over to the idea that dogs can learn a great deal when they are very young. Simple commands and hand signals became quickly imprinted upon the young dog.

Roy shortened that winter for us, if such a thing is possible in Minnesota. He became a focal-point, a goal, sometimes even an excuse: "We need to get going so we can let the dog out." He became a reflex—as we entered the house we immediately let him out. Either he was gradually becoming a bit human or we were becoming a bit canine. As our children came in the door, he greeted each of them with the wagging tail and the bright dog-smile that seemed to almost be human. If he wasn't there the first words said by whoever entered the door were, "Where's Roy?"

It was a six-week commitment. Every Wednesday night we took Roy to puppy class. It was all about socialization with other people and other dogs. There were lectures about feeding and housebreaking, dog health issues, and various dog accessories. I don't think the scheduled commitment affected Roy nearly as much as it did Jenessa and me. We agreed to team up and adjust our busy schedules to get the pup to all of the classes.

Roy was always happy to go. Anytime he could ride in the vehicle and go somewhere, he was excited. It didn't take more than a couple of sessions and he seemed to know where we were going, and his anticipation of the sights and smells of puppy class was easily detected. He'd get very hyper when he realized it was "class-night" and we'd always figure he'd somehow forget all his training and make us look like idiots who couldn't get their pup to learn and behave.

The most remarkable part was that after we arrived, and he had gotten his "fix" of all the wonderful scents and sounds, he actually settled down for the class. He seemed to revel in the competition. One memorable night after nearly pulling me headfirst down the steps to the auditorium, then cavorting with a stylish young female springer spaniel before class and tangling leashes with a young German shepherd, he then settled down and sat perfectly upon command. Immediately after that Roy heeled upon command and we proudly stepped across the auditorium in perfect rhythm and synchronization. I began to detect his ability to be one kind of dog one moment and a totally differently behaving dog the next moment. As later training commenced it became more evident he could be a laid back Lab at certain times and a fireball of enthusiasm when he needed to be. He was not to be a dog-like robotic machine. He operated on heart and emotion. There were times when his independence allowed him to nearly perform miracles—at other times it was to frustrate me to no end.

The puppy training was low-key and filled with positive reinforcement and treats. Yet the puppy training built all the essentials into the dog. All the basics like "sit," "come," "heel," and "stay," were taught. We worked with him a lot, and with him in the house with us constantly, training took place almost continuously in little bits and pieces.

I recall coming home from the classes and realizing that mental work tired a dog far more than physical exertion. As we'd sit down in the living room to watch TV or visit, he'd sprawl on the rug, totally exhausted. He was limp with fatigue and his eyes would roll back in his head. You could move his soft little paws around and he would just lie there. Soon those little jerks and almost inaudible little sounds would be evident. The pure joy of a sleeping, contented dog on the floor sometimes overwhelmed me. There was so much watching, training, and correcting. A pup can be tiring and so I always told everyone to "let a sleeping dog lie."

Each day he followed me to my office and soon took the habit of lying under my computer desk. During that first winter, he was a welcome foot-warmer as he dozed on top of my feet. My wife left for work early and I spent quiet work time alone with my little foot-warmer before other employees arrived. My pair of slip-on boots would come off at the door and my little furry foot-warmer would be waiting under my desk. The secure space under my desk became more important to Roy than the kennel-box where he slept at night or when we were gone. As I write this I miss the cozy warmth, the softness, and sleepy contentment of my sleeping dog.

Somehow the peace and solitude of that sleeping dog gave me a sense of contentment. I wondered if it was Roy or

I who benefited more from his quiet time on the living room rug. Sometimes I hated to wake him because it was time for him to go to his box for the night, so we could go to bed. In later years our box became his, as he eventually moved into our bedroom where he slept by our bed each night for the better part of nine years. Just the contented, warm, mound of fur brought joy.

Even now, I get up at night and look to step over my dog. Of course he's not there, only the phantom-dog who seems to never leave the place near the bed. Sometimes my bare feet seem to detect that warm spot on the carpet where Roy slept. Our tracks crossed and re-crossed as Roy learned from us and we learned from him.

Those last nights during the fall of 2010, he lay there, panting and ravaged by the relentless hunger associated with his condition, yet even then he would calm, and his breathing would ease. I saw that pup, so contented, legs twitching, little sounds telling me of dog-dreams, of hunts relived or perhaps just dreaming about the joy of being stretched out under my computer desk.

Nothing like a warm puppy on the rug.

13

3

It would be the summer of heavy lifting in the dog training arena. Roy was growing fast and now the outside training was becoming very important. Spring had erupted from the ice and snow. We have the long season of snow and ice-covered frozen ground and then it all blossoms into the season of mud. Sending four little paws outside to go potty in the springtime can be a very dangerous proposition. Those little paws can find a lot of sludge to run through on a bathroom run.

Roy, of course, was a Labrador retriever, a breed well known for its love of water and all things associated with water. Fortunately we had grass for him to visit on his daily forays outside, and, remarkably, he always seemed fastidious about staying out of muddy places. Don't get me wrong, in later years he tramped through countless marshes, and traversed incredibly harsh and muddy places in all kinds of weather, never seeming to mind any of it. Yet, he meticulously cleaned his feet and fur when around the house, and always seemed to avoid getting his feet dirty as much as possible. Perhaps the rogue/royalty breeding really had some credence.

All retriever breeds are incredible in their desire to retrieve. These dogs will perform almost any task if somehow it leads to bringing things back to their master. Much training revolves around the retrieve, and using that instinct to teach other commands. Retrievers will sit, stay, heel, or perform any number of other commands, if at the end of those commands they will be able to fetch.

Teaching Roy to retrieve was a very ego-building endeavor for me. I assume it also helped Roy's self-esteem, if indeed self-esteem is something dogs are aware of. As I recall the retrieve-training, it seems all of his ability came naturally, and all I needed to do was let him be himself. His first retrieve was a tennis ball, and he was very young, perhaps only eight weeks or so. He loved the tennis ball, and it was easy to roll it around and get him excited about chasing it. The retrieve part was easy, because I just rolled the ball down a hallway. He chased it and when he caught it I clapped and called him. He, of course, had the ball in his mouth and there was no way he could get past me, so I gently stopped him and told him to sit. Then I took the ball as I said "drop." It was easy, because he wanted to give it to me so I would roll it again. It soon became second nature for him to just bring it to me so we could play the game again.

Roy taught me a lot that summer. He showed me what an amazing bond can be built with a leash. I had always thought of a leash as only a way to restrain or control a dog, yet it serves a much greater purpose. It becomes a bridge between dog and master. The leash is a relationship-builder that is special.

The ears perked up, and upon the "click" that announced the leash in place, Roy went on duty. His attention turned to me and the expectant look of "what's the assignment" came upon his face. Now we were one. We became a unit that could maneuver through commands and tasks. Corrections became less necessary as he anticipated what needed to be done.

He showed no hatred of the leash, but on the contrary, he now felt he owned me completely. No one or anything could come between us. Roy never believed anything other, than he owned me, he believed he was the leader, and I only the facilitator of his actions. *How quickly can I perform the command, how often can I elicit positive comments?* seemed to be his motivation. I began to understand that he wanted me happy, he wanted to please.

The bonding was taking place, just as surely as that first wolf entered the circle of firelight near his ancient master, and designated that man as his pack leader, learned to hunt with that man, and share the spoils. With us the leash was only the facilitator of an invisible bond, and leash or no leash, the cooperation remained. The leash was a way to get the dog to know what was expected, what the response should be to a command. Words soon transferred and took the place of a leash to a great extent.

The exhilarating, but at times, humbling experience of the dog-master relationship emerged. Now the real work began. The challenge became one of somehow crossing the barrier of understanding. If he could know what I wanted, he wanted to do it. Perhaps it was the following that helped him know. Each day he did what I did. If my project was to build a door on a greenhouse, he followed me to get the tools, he watched as I sawed boards or fastened materials with screws. He could lie and watch me perform tasks that should have bored him to tears. I think I was his subject, his bridge to some understanding of what makes humans tick.

Both children and dogs go through stages of growing up.

So I did at times wonder "What is time to a dog?" His patience with me was unequaled, and I marveled at his desire to just watch me do things that had no relevance to him or any instinct he possessed.

To be certain, his enthusiasm peaked when he followed me to the field when I was carrying a retrieving dummy. As training progressed I brought out something that made that loud noise that signaled there would soon be a retrieve. Oh, he loved the gun and reveled in its loud noise, for things fell from the sky at its report, and those things needed retrieving. What joy! He would follow me all day through endless boring projects, if only to follow for a half hour of training and retrieving.

Fortunately, we had learned to introduce the sound of the gun gradually to the pup. We started with cap guns at feeding time and gradually advanced to the sound of a shotgun. Of course the ever-loved retrieve was a positive reinforcement to the loud sound. The report of a gun soon became the best sound the dog could hope to hear. I remember the old school theory of my older dog-training mentors who believed that a dog either was okay with the sound of a gun or was gun-shy. The idea back then was to shoot a shotgun over a young dog to see how he reacted. If he got scared and ran away he was pronounced gun-shy and deemed useless as a hunting dog. My guess was that a lot of potentially talented dogs were abandoned because they just were not acclimated to loud noises and probably could've been. Dog training in the old days was much less of a positive experience for dogs, and more of a do-or-die thing. Either a dog had what it took or he was deemed of no value. Certainly discipline and correction are important in all training, and to be sure Roy needed plenty of both. Fortunately his spirit was such that even after correction he came back with his tail wagging, ready to try again.

The following, the growing presence of a shadow, the emerging assurance of solid allegiance, crept into my consciousness. He was always there, becoming a part of each day. He followed me down the aisles between the plant benches in the greenhouse. Of course he could scamper under the expanded metal, table-like plant holders. He would run and explore underneath the low tables. As he grew, there became less clearance under those benches, until one morning as he scampered along, I heard a sudden howling scream from under the plant benches. Out he came, back into the aisle where I saw blood running from the top of his head. Roy had grown enough so he couldn't run and jump under those plant benches anymore. He had paid the price of growing larger, with a gaping gouge inflicted by a sharp point, perhaps a screw that protruded from the structure he had been so accustomed to running under.

The gouge left a scar on his right forehead, a permanent identification mark. After that day, he began to travel only the walking aisles like the rest of us.

There are so many things for a puppy to learn when he is less than a year old. I am amazed that puppies survive their first year. One of my greatest fears for pups is that they will have a fatal run-in with a vehicle. As cars moved near, whenever we were outside with the dog, I instinctively yelled, "no." Many stories of good dogs being run over and killed reminded me of the immediate danger of cars and dogs. I was young, maybe third grade, and a friend had a young German short-haired pup. The pup simply ran out into the street and collided with a car. No loud sound, no brakes, just the dull thud of rubber against a furry little pup. Years later my cousin's father-in-law, a devoted 'coon hunter, told of his prize black-and-tan hound, hot on the trail of a raccoon when the 'coon crossed a busy highway. The hound bounded across the road in hot pursuit, only to be hit fatally by a passing car. I kept the vision of countless dogs lying alongside of numerous highways as we passed, their collars still vivid in my mind with shining studs on black leather—lifeless dogs fallen victim to cars.

Each time I let my dog out to go potty, I watched and tried to keep him under control. Soon the days of puppy-hood and constant leashes waned, and I knew we needed to allow this dog to run without a leash or a check cord. Now he was corrected only by the invisible bond of trust and command. If we failed in our control, or he failed to respond, disaster could result. Much as we let go of our children, we let the physical controls wane and more and more trusted the governance of heart and mind. Only when this dog is allowed to run free, can he attain his full potential. There will be times when he must run on his own instinct and ability, to be the best he can be. His nose and instinct are far more advanced than mine and I must allow him his freedom to be able to utilize his in-born potential.

Now only the following mattered, only the ancient bonds of man and canine. These became the bonds that protect and enhance dog and man. The boundaries needed to be explored, yet always the look back, the eye contact that enabled my input, my signal, my command. Voice commands gradually transferred to hand signals. Long check cords reinforced commands and soon the check cords also had to be abandoned, for the following had to become an action of will.

His following never stopped. Even that last day, he followed as best he could. Shaky legs, limping upon infection-inflamed limbs, he followed me, as I moved about the house. As I coaxed him out into snow-covered grass to pee and back up laborious steps into the door, he followed—some of the most difficult following of his life. The parted hair still showed that scar on the right side of his forehead: a long-past injury of learning and following. So much following, some rewarded only by pain and disappointment, yet the hope and optimism still seemed embedded in those eyes, for much of the following had led to joy. He had followed me to distant destinations, to golden fields and duck-filled marshes. We had traveled to many great destinations, and now we would travel to the last destination.

4

H e wants to go with you," Muriel called after me. The dog had his nose pressed against the door, fogging the glass, ears at high attention, and eyes darting from me to the truck.

"I'm just going into town to the bank."

"Let him go along."

And so it began by placing him up on the front seat. Of course he immediately climbed onto my lap, and I gently moved him over on the seat. Each time he attempted to move on to me as I drove, I moved him back onto the middle of the seat.

I remember how he finally lay down on the seat and stared up at me with hurt eyes—*How can you keep me way over here?* Soon he edged closer, crept with incremental moves until his little muzzle lay upon my right leg. His gaze was all-knowing, seeming to say, *You can't possibly ostracize me completely.* And so he rode, head resting upon my leg, content to be close to me.

The fixation upon my truck had begun. The center of the seat was his. He knew I sat behind the steering wheel, but the next seat over was his. Either he sat up on the seat or he lay with his head upon my leg.

I pulled up to the teller's window at the drive through at the bank. It was late on a Friday and the teller frowned as she picked up my transaction from the tray. A terse "Thank-you," and just as she began completing our banking she glanced up to peer into the truck cab. The rigid face melted upon seeing the little perk-eared fluff-ball sitting upright on the seat next to me. She stopped her paced counting and cheerily asked, "What's his name?"

"Roy," I replied.

"How cute," the rushed brusqueness of her demeanor melted and she seemed calmed.

"Can he have a treat?"

"Yeah."

As the receipt came back, there was a little Milk-Bone holding it down in the metal drawer. Roy's usual curious nose picked up on the treat immediately and his reaction brought a big smile from the frazzled teller.

Now here was a new game Roy could really get in to. Whenever we went through a drive through of any kind from then on he got excited. The truck was his special friend, it was a place to sit next to me, to be a sort of equal pack-mate as well as capitalize on the occasional treat.

Whenever we walked past the truck he'd stop and stare at the door, gaze up and try to convince me that we needed to take a ride. Everything associated with the truck was positive for him. In the summer, the cool air from the air conditioner felt good to a panting dog. In the winter, the warmth lulled him to sleep on the soft seat. Sometimes a treat awaited him on a trip to the bank. The truck was his passport to all sorts of adventures and new experiences.

As he got older he was trained to jump into his kennel box in the back of the truck. This was a necessity when he later traveled to faraway hunting destinations, yet he always felt the back of the truck was a demotion.

"Shall we ride in the truck?" I'd say and he'd always get excited and run to the vehicle. He always went to the driver's side door and stood there expectantly. When I opened the back and said "kennel," his head drooped and he walked slowly to the back. Indeed he really came to not like getting into the back. When another person got into the front and he was forced to ride in the back, it was a direct assault on his position in the pack.

Sometimes Muriel and I both rode in the truck and Roy was allowed to sit between us. Those were his most special times in the truck. I guess he really felt he had reached equality at those times, sitting right up between the two major figures of authority in his life. If he wasn't sitting, he would have his head resting on my knee, certain that control of the vehicle rested solely in his paws.

As the yellow Lab became older, he actually became very protective of my truck. I remember a spot of sunlight brightened the red-and-black cloth front seat of my truck. Short blond hair stuck to the fabric and had become a permanent part of the seat. The new improvised pseudo-den, the "place" assigned in the truck now took on the special meaning of places that needed to be protected, secured only for special pack-mates. The need to stake out territory was fulfilled by that wrinkled front seat of the Chevy pick-up.

There seem to be a few sacred places in a dog's mind. The holy of holies: the kennel box, later the master's bedroom, and now the front seat of my truck. Those special square feet of the planet, not allowed to be violated, meant to be protected by some single-minded retriever, were coming into focus for the young dog. Some ethereal gene, long since passed on to the Labrador tribe, now manifest in the special front seat fabric of my truck.

He was a couple of years old and it was the time of year that allowed windows to be open as one drove in a vehicle. Roy had become a fixture on the seat beside me in the pick-up. It was the kind of day that caused him to pant—wide pink tongue lolling and dripping dog-sweat. There was always a kind of attentiveness, eyes flashing from side to side, catching each movement as people walked, and other vehicles surged and merged.

The road construction slowed us, typical of most summer days in our section of the construction season. I relaxed when we slowed to a stop, elbow stuck out the open window, eyes intent upon the car ahead, when a movement to my left caught my attention.

"Can you tell me how to get to Fifth Street?" The voice of the movement shouted as a man came close to my open window. At the same instant, a tan shadow burst across the seat and a flash of barred teeth went past me and to the open window. The man stopped in his tracks, waved, and backed away, apparently deciding he could get those directions from some other stopped vehicle.

"Sit," I jerked Roy's collar and put him back into his space on the seat beside me. Roy gave little quarter to anyone messing with the truck-space. Certainly, he surprised me into a new sense of alertness, and the realization that I needed to be extra cautious about vehicle etiquette. Roy kept me extremely conscientious of traffic laws, for I always feared getting pulled over for speeding or running a stop-light and having the dog attack an officer. Fantasy scenarios of my dog being shot with a service revolver danced in my mind. I knew I could never stop his protective ardor for the truck. I also knew that if someone were to ride in the truck who wasn't family, I needed to let them in first, so that Roy could enter the truck after them and invade their space. He never had a problem with anyone who I had previously authorized to be in the truck. It was always a matter of invading his space, because anyone could call him over to their space and have no problem.

Call him over to you and you can pet him, and all will be well, but woe to anyone who invades the sacred area. If we were settled into our bedroom at night and anyone walked into our door, they were greeted with a most unfriendly growl. Call him out and all is fine, for then you can come in and he will follow with docile deference. The split personality of docile, happy, friendly Labrador, laced with a bit of the old protective retriever mentality was evident.

As we began to realize the great talent, and the innate intelligence of Roy, we began to wonder if someday we might want a puppy from him, but the protectiveness caused us not to want the gene passed on, and convinced us that in later years, as we became blessed with grandchildren, we wanted to be very careful not to have another dog that was so protective. I suppose the greatest force in our decision to get Roy neutered went back to the protective trait. If only we could assure the loyalty, the talent, and the loving spirit of the dog, without the possibility of his offspring being ready to take the leg off anyone who invaded his space, we would have opted to let those genetics propagate.

When we were out in the field both dog and master were freed of our flaws. I would give the sit command, and with body quivering, tense with desire to retrieve, he was ready to move forward with the assignment. These were the times our spirits melded and we longed to please, to keep our bargain with each other. Later all would lead to the shot, and then the waited-for words, the anticipation beyond all anticipations—the word "fetch."

This word he knew to be the real thing, the culmination of all the training, all the bonding, all the emergence to the surface of his being, of instincts dating back long before any memory. "Fetch," the word that pushed all protectiveness to the farthest corner of his consciousness, the word that destroyed any animosity with any person, the word, along with the circumstance that Roy lived for, and even in the dimness of his last days the word that would have cleared his mind, and driven him to do super-dog feats. There was no protectiveness on the retrieve, for it was the time to "give," to swell with pride and transfer pride to the master as well.

We got past the protectiveness. We learned to avoid the situation and the areas. It required great attentiveness, but he was a dog far beyond those little spots in his world. Those protected spots diminished during his last days. The special spot on the rug was relinquished. Those who helped him, attended to him, could come into his space, and he knew they meant to take nothing from him. Yet, the spot on the truck seat remained special until the end. The last day I lifted his shivering body up to the seat. He looked up at the seat from the ground, he lifted a front paw to the floor-board, to tell me he really wanted to ride up front. His legs splayed as I put my arms under his chest and stomach and placed him onto the seat.

We drove and he struggled to sit up, to see the road, the white ditches where he seemed to know the roosters hid. He lay down again and edged to my leg. It was and always was his most cherished spot—me driving, he resting upon my leg, sprawled out on his most protected spot on earth. There was a kind of peace for him as he rode with me that last time in the truck.

🐾5🐾

The first summer began to ripen the little dog's traits. As the sun burned green lines into the landscape, he strengthened and grew. The summer here in the North will brown us and lull us into a deep-seated complacency. The feeling of never-ending days, dark to light but a short time, squeezed between the broad smile of sunlight. Time after working was still filled with hours of light to build a dog if that is what one desires. In the field he was released from protecting his sacred spaces. Perhaps we all are freed from the burden of protectiveness. Maybe it's born into all of us the same as it's born into retrievers. As we protect our little spaces such as family, business, and home, the little Labrador, too, learned to protect certain areas of his life.

The summer freed us all as we ran and learned and crossed each other's boundaries. Yet even as a long summer stretched before us, how could we pack so much into it? The formative time seemed fleeting, perhaps too short to squeeze in everything that needed to be done. There were the basic commands to build upon, and reinforce. Beyond those skills were the leash, the long check cord, the gun conditioning, and of course the crowning activity of the summer was gun dog school. In this course he would be introduced to birds and all the wonderful things associated with his profession. Now, all the investment into the specialized instrument attached to the end of his face would be tested and honed. Yes, his nose would be trained. He would begin to use it effectively to differentiate the smells he needed to be interested in and those he needed to ignore. Now, the true talent of the Labrador would be focused as we began to point out to him the scents we wanted him to remember.

We had sent him to kindergarten which was puppy school. We had gone on to elementary school with basic obedience training, and now his higher education would begin with bird-dog school.

Yes, it was bird-dog class and he was so ready. There was no messing around here. We assembled in the auditorium and he sat at attention because he sensed the awesome nature of the assemblage. He knew there were birds and retrieving dummies. "Sit" and "stay" were old hat—no problem, let me at it. I knew it was all in his heart, passed along from generations of his breed. We only needed to release the actions in the proper sequence to get it right.

Roy knew Mandy, the instructor, for she had worked with us in obedience training and he knew to respect her. She held the key to retrieving. Somehow he knew she also held the key to the fulfillment of his dog-dreams.

I remember Butch, the big yellow Labrador next to us, as we listened to Mandy's instructions. He allowed no one to get into his space, growling and baring his teeth. He nipped a dog next to him and Mandy warned Butch and his master. If it happened one more time, Butch was out of there. Despite all of his innate ability, he would not be trained in this class. She tolerated no dogs that might bite or fight. Roy had his protective places, but out in the public area of training he remained docile and compliant. We knew this was the big deal. Roy wanted what was here. The excellence of his nose and his inherent instincts became very apparent, and Mandy immediately told us he had talent.

I have never seen a more intense reaction to live birds than that of Roy as he saw and smelled, and heard the real feathered quarry, and later as he mouthed and tasted the soft, sweet real birds. Never have I seen such intensity; every muscle in his body tensed and shook, yet discipline ruled and I knew the obedience training had been good. There was controlled speed, steel muscles, tempered with discipline of the working dog. Predispositions from an ancient and dim past now surfaced in the most remarkable display of performance.

I had learned that having a dog is borderline marriage. It pretty much turns out to be for better or worse. When you raise a pup it doesn't take long for attachment to set in. Over the years, I've had a number of dogs. They all had redeeming characteristics, and most had flaws. A lot of flaws are probably self-imposed by the master because they are caused by flaws in our training or conditioning of the pup.

It's a dangerous thing to get a puppy. Before you really are fully aware of his potential, he has grabbed your heart, and your children have fallen in love with him. There is no turning back and even though you know that the maintenance far exceeds the initial cost, even a less-than-perfect dog will stay.

Dogs have a way of edging close to the home fire and taking whatever you toss their way, all the while making you guilty for giving them so little. Yet, so often you feel that just maybe, the next dog will be perfect, he will have all the assets to balance all the flaws of past dogs.

We finished the classes in the field, real conditions of thick cover and real birds. Roy handled his first pheasant with the excited yet gentle lips of the retriever breed. Live birds, unhurt by the dog, were delivered to me and given to my hand.

I began to believe that Roy was truly my golden boy, possibly one of the best dogs with which I'd ever hunted. The way he watched and marked the downed bird, and the way he retrieved to hand, sitting and giving in such perfect form made my heart skip a beat.

I had worked with many dogs, companions of my youth. These were dogs that led me through the golden fields of my younger days and together we followed the feathered quarry through the years. These were meat-dogs, possessing the raw instinct of their various breeds. They flushed, pointed, and retrieved their way through life, and each one carries special memories. Although their instincts were sound, they all had habits that were less than perfect. Why did Butch insist upon burying the downed birds that he found in the field?

There were hard-mouthed dogs that retrieved but were not kind to the potential table-quality of the retrieved birds. I had seen fragments of the raw instinct in my dogs before. We had allowed such instinct to suffice in these dogs and worked with them, taking what they had to offer. My dad always said that any dog was better than none at all. In the days of my youth, many bird hunters didn't have dogs and having one always gave an advantage. The adult mentors of those days pretty much believed that either a dog had it or he didn't. The dog had to be a natural at hunting and retrieving or he was not deemed worthy of his feed. These were folks who grew up with little, and had come through the Great Depression. Dogs were culled and only the ones with real talent were kept around. They probably didn't require as much training to be good at their job.

My guess is that some of those dogs were exceptional, yet really didn't get a lot of formal training. It was mostly on-the-job training under real field conditions. From a strictly genetic point of view, those old days were probably good for building a line of inherently talented dogs. Any dogs not top-notch were quickly culled and weren't bred. There were no correction collars to force mediocre dogs to perform. Either the dog had genetic talent or he was not kept. With the advanced training systems of today, dogs with less gifted abilities are still rendered acceptable dogs and some are bred which really have sub-par talent.

I think that every dog is a mulligan, a do-over. With each dog there is the optimism and hope for perfection. Roy filled the bill. He loved the various types of cover, hunted and used his nose and instincts to complete the tasks. He learned to quarter and work the cover thoroughly, moved like he'd been doing it for years. The realization dawned on me one day, that he was less than a year old and already he knew the skills and understood the discipline required to be really good at his job. The memory of the rank enthusiasm that possessed the rapidly growing yellow dog still is etched in my mind.

Those were the long days of a first summer, promising so much to come. They were the days of hot work, and crazy, busy schedules. Our business was at its peak in those summer months. Our kids had many activities that demanded our attention, and yet each day, after its furious pace, demanded that the last part of that day be filled with retrieving dummies, check cords, and whistle commands that probably caused neighbors to suspect some kind of outdoor basketball tournament was happening in our field.

"I'll set some scented retrieving dummies in the tall grass," I told my daughter. "Then you can bring Roy through the area and have him find them."

New games were always being created, different ways to train, unique distractions to try to get the pup off task, so we could correct him and reinforce the proper response or behavior.

Each day I saw traffic go by and feared he'd get caught on the road by a passing vehicle. Yet each day I grew a bit more confident that he was becoming more focused and better able to be controlled, and saved from possible tragedy.

Roy began to use all his senses, and now didn't just follow me but began to lead. He was a dominant creature, and never wanted to be left behind. He knew that when we were in the field his place was up front. After all the following, he now began to determine his own tracks, to lead me to follow him when the situation demanded.

"Heel," I'd command and he'd reluctantly fall back. How proudly he'd walk at my side, yet I knew he wanted to break, he really wanted to get out in front. He'd flow in liquid motion, moving with such ease through various types of terrain. Watching him work the fields always was such a joy. Maybe it was a sort of newness, or maybe a renewal for me, but his quartering through the fields was a great and new triumph for me.

I never imagined on those warm sunny afternoons of his first year, that I'd squint to imagine and re-live his perfect harmony on a cold snowy November day twelve years later. Then, even in his weakness, there was a sureness of foot, a practiced movement that even in perfect health couldn't be duplicated by any other creature. He quartered on that last cold day and I imagined a pup, not shackled by the throes of illness, but all heart, knowing full well it was bird season and there was a certain hope in the knowing.

W hat is cold, wet, black, and smells?" I asked.
"Roy's nose," my bright young daughter replied.
One of the first things that drew me to the little pup, as we watched and decided which one to take home, was his endless sniffing, his relentless search for something. The little black unit on the end of his face was his most golden asset. We knew the genetics were promising. Both his parents were exceptional hunters and we expected the puppy to have inherited those characteristics.

It is true all dogs can smell a thousand times better than humans, and can detect a scent that is one million times less concentrated than anything humans can sense. With 220 million receptors in his nose, we paid just one cent per 22,000 receptors. Yet, our investment in that nose grew rapidly as we fed and cared for our dog.

The sensitivity of a dog's nose is truly a miracle, and the hyper-selectivity of the Labrador's nose is beyond belief. It is no wonder they can be trained to find certain things such as drugs or explosives. I'll never forget the time when I was traveling in an area where fruit was strictly forbidden to be brought into the area, because of a fruit disease quarantine. As I stood near a traveling companion at the airport, my friend's suitcase was viciously attacked by a black Labrador retriever who was employed by the Agriculture Department to enforce fruit importation rules.

"May I have a look in your bag?" the inspector asked. Sure enough, there was a forgotten apple tucked into the suitcase. It is a bit unsettling to have your luggage attacked by a dog, but I was amazed at how the dog picked out the scent of an apple from all the myriad of smells in the airport.

I have tried to imagine what it must be like to have such a powerful sense of smell. I have watched dogs put their noses right next to some pretty nasty smelling things, and can only imagine what it would be like to smell those things a thousand times more intensely. I've decided that no smell must be unpleasant to a dog or they would spend their lives dodging many different things.

Of course, the ability to pick out a certain scent and pursue it is the instinct that most excites trainers who work with dogs. We too, would try to cultivate the selective ability in our new pup. Again I must hark back to my Dad's thoughts on dogs: "They'll learn to hunt whatever you want them to hunt." By that he meant that if you pursue pheasants and shoot the ones the dog flushes, he will know that is the scent you are interested in following. By ignoring rabbits and telling the dog "no" on that scent he learns to exclude it from his nasal repertoire. Of course there is some ancestral breeding that begins to separate bird-dogs from 'coon-hounds, but Labradors seem so anxious to please their masters, that they can be taught to respond to almost any scent.

When Roy came home, we of course had to know how good his nose could smell. Soon he learned to like the little Milk-Bone treats we used to reinforce his training and we soon devised a way to test and sharpen his nose.

"Take Roy in the other room," I said. When he was in another room, I'd take a Milk-Bone and drag it across the living room in an undulating pattern until I finally hid it under a piece of furniture.

"Bring him back in now."

We put him onto the beginning of the trail. Immediately his tail began to fan excitedly as he smelled something he loved. He soon learned to follow the sweet trail on the rug to the treat. The little puff-ball was only half knee-high and already was trailing. My impression of the dog's nose grew immensely. I could hardly believe how the little guy could already hunt.

Of course our goal was not to create a Milk-Bone retriever, and we soon transferred the ability to other scents. As he became older it was easy to put pheasant scent onto a retrieving dummy and drag it through the weeds for him to follow.

One thing we come to learn as we work with dogs is that we really have to trust in their noses. We humans assume we know more than our dogs because we are the 'masters' and they are the dogs. Yet in the nose department, the dog is infinitely superior. Roy continued to reinforce these lessons with me, time and again over the years.

There is a point when a dog is working, where you must let him lead, and he always leads with his nose. Roy's nose was very smart. He learned very quickly that there were short cuts to finding the quarry. He had learned to follow the Milk-Bone trail as it zigzagged across the living room rug and he learned to follow the trail of bird scent that formed a tortuous path through grass and tall weeds. As he matured, he began to use the wind. I saw the nose go up and the tortuous path to the quarry was shortened as the wind currents wafted the scent straight to him when he got down-wind of the bird. Roy's greatest asset, his pinnacle of common sense was achieved on that day when

Blond kids.

his nose went up as he followed the trail. Now he proceeded straight to the quarry. The wind brought the hot, rich scent of the bird directly to him.

Roy had learned the magic of the wind. He knew that everything up-wind of him could be read and interpreted by his miraculous nose. Soon the wind meant more to Roy than the sound of food hitting his dish. As he approached the front door first thing in the morning, his first instinct was to raise his nose and check the wind. There would be no step forward until the air currents were checked, and he knew everything that was out there. I soon knew him as a "nose-up" dog, always trusting the air. One of the things that marked his transition from puppy-hood to adult-hood was the newly assumed position of his nose.

We had our disputes in later years as we hunted together. Roy could never understand why anyone would ever want to travel anywhere going with the wind. Of course, I always tried to hunt against the wind, but it's hard to return to your vehicle without traveling with the wind at least some of the time.

When we were forced to move with the wind, Roy always wanted to get up ahead and then work back, using the wind to his advantage. I've since come to believe that all dogs have great nasal attributes, but some use these natural gifts better than others. Roy seemed to usually "hunt smart," using the wind and the terrain to his greatest advantage.

Roy, in later years, became my cattail dog. We often hunted the edges of large marshes where there were dry, un-flooded cattails, that bordered the wetter areas of the marsh. Pheasants were often to be found in these dry edges, and even out into the wet areas of the marsh. All I needed to do was walk down the edge of these areas on the down-wind side of the marsh and take Roy with me. He merely moved along the edge of these areas walking relatively easy and kept his nose up. I knew if he stopped and moved out into the reeds and heavy cover a pheasant would soon flush. He seemed to have a long range when he got down wind of the birds. With a bit of a breeze he could cover nearly a hundred yards and seemingly never miss a bird.

The selectiveness of his nose also became apparent as he got older and he seemed to be able to differentiate between hen and rooster pheasants. He knew we didn't shoot the hens and learned to ignore them in favor of the roosters, which he knew were candidates for retrieving. I don't know if hens and roosters actually smell differently, or if the roosters just have a more intense scent and are differentiated because of the difference in the amount of scent given off by the bird.

I learned to always take him on the down-wind side of patches of cover and felt confident we covered the area by just hitting its edge. Roy liked to do things as easy as they could be done, not wanting to crash through a lot of extra cover if he didn't need to do it.

If his nose was his greatest asset, at times it also became a problem. Roy never needed to trail game on the ground, he always took the short cut and followed his nose straight to the bird. For him the shortest route was great, for me it meant I needed to get there more quickly, and he became less easy to follow, as he became faster at trailing. I really needed to learn to anticipate where the bird might be hiding and also anticipate Roy's actions.

I now know why God put a dog's nose on his most forward part. A canine leads with his nose. It's the first point of contact with anything he meets. The dog evaluates and decides upon his response based upon the first whiff of whatever and whoever he meets. Roy taught me, more than any other dog, what a powerful instrument a dog's nose can be. I watched him follow what I thought were impossible trails, cold trails, trails through extremely difficult terrain, and trails I never dreamed existed. He could leave a bone or chew toy in some obscure place, yet find it days later. He even developed a memory, something that is not supposed to be an asset of a dog. I believe his memory rested more in his nose than in his brain. Certain smells in an area triggered recollections of what he had left there.

Roy's other senses certainly complimented his sense of smell. I soon learned that Roy was an extremely visual dog. We began to train him with hand signals that were always tied to a verbal command. Of course he learned to take hand signals just as readily as verbal commands. We spent so much time together that Roy always watched me. He looked for hand signals and visual signs of what to next expect.

One evening a new realization about his sense of sight and comprehension became apparent. As he lay on the living room rug, I looked at him and I smiled. Immediately upon smiling he began to thump and wag his tail. I began to realize he actually reacted to my facial expressions. A stern look would stop him and his ears would perk up, perhaps anticipating a command or a reprimand. I am certain he could have been given commands by merely winking if such served any practical purpose.

When you both live and work with a dog, you become connected on a higher level. Just as a dog begins to anticipate your next action when you change clothes, or get dressed in a certain way the dog becomes anxious because he knows you are getting ready to leave. When you're in the field and you begin to move in a certain direction, or point to an area of cover to be investigated the dog knows to go in that direction.

Communication between Roy and me became quite instinctive. The slightest movement and Roy knew what was next, whether it involved being fed, or going out the door to the office. I have always been amazed at how few actual commands needed to be given as Roy became older. We seemed to reach a point of mutual understanding. He knew what was expected, and what he was not allowed to do.

He lay on the hallway rug between the bedroom and the bathroom, his brown eyes following my every move.

Stretched with his head on his front paws, he had a far-away-gaze in his eyes. It was a winter morning and a trip out to the office was the best outcome he could imagine.

Perhaps some ancient recollection, burned into his DNA from a thousand years past, faintly grazed his brain as he lay there on the rug. There was the hard feel of hugging frozen ground and the veil of brush and tall-grass cover as he hovered with ears flattened. Only his nose was alive and processing scents far beyond the view of his slowly sweeping eyes. The ancient dog was wolf-like in his patience that some quarry would move near and into striking distance. Far away in the nether-past Roy journeyed, and lay in ambush on the hallway rug until "let's go" broke his canine reverie and he followed me down the stairs and out the door onto the shoveled sidewalk.

There's a special bond that develops between all dog-lovers and their best canine friends. For the hunter and his dog it takes on a special emotion, for we are not just friends but working partners. The human side of the partnership surrenders to the nose of the canine, knowing it is something Man can never possess and only through the dog can he vicariously experience the sense of smell of a dog. Each move, each change of direction telegraphs to the master what the dog smells, and in turn what the quarry is doing, what it has in its mind, how it plans its escape.

The dog too knows the bond, for he is totally dependent upon the human for the final joy of the hunt. The good dogs learn early, the lesson of the dim past. Somehow they know the surrender that took place eons ago as that first young wolf crept into the fire light of the human. The acceptance of that scrap of meat or tasty bone was the beginning. Forsaking the killing power of his pack, that first reckless canine gave in to a new bond. How strange and wonderful the relationship—giving man access to the wonders of the canine nose and fusing it to the power of the human intellect. The tracks of dog and man began to merge and part into a pattern of cooperation. Sometimes the dog-tracks led and at other times they followed.

The bonds between us and our dogs are deep-seated in the dim and aged past. The connections are deep. I felt these connections more deeply than ever in the last day that Roy lay upon my rug. I watched as some of his senses dimmed. My hand signals became veiled and clouded, maybe recognized only by intuition, sometimes misread altogether. Sounds and commands, once clear and easily acted upon, became distant and less meaningful as pain and fatigue distracted his day. Yet the black, pulsing bit of skin and fiber at the end of his face never stopped. He still knew every square inch of his environment and every other creature near and far by the intellect of his nose. His nose never let him down, it never let me down, and it could have followed me much longer, had the rest of him survived.

7

I wonder if when a dog travels, his distances are in regular miles or dog miles. At times in the fall of the year as we tramp the fields in search of the elusive pheasant or grouse we will clock thirty miles or more per day on our pedometers. I've always felt that a hunting dog probably puts on twice the miles of his human companion, as the dog quarters back and forth across the cover and veers off to investigate promising areas of tall grass or brush. I would imagine that estimating sixty miles a day for the dog would not be an exaggeration. Of course that's four hundred and twenty miles a day in dog miles since we are taught to multiply a dog's age by seven when calculating his dog years. It's no wonder our dogs tend to lay at our feet at night and sleep the deep sleep of exhaustion.

Over his career Roy probably put on nearly 208,000 dog miles hunting, which is the equivalent of over eight times around the earth or nearly the distance one would need to walk to get to the moon. Of course some of those miles were spent in the water retrieving game downed over marshes or ponds, and I'm not even adding in the miles logged during training. It's hard to imagine logging all of those miles without even wearing shoes. I actually bought him a pair of shoes, which in reality were leather doggie-boots to protect his feet in areas where we hunted that had a lot of prickly pear cactus. Roy did not like them at all and after the nearly impossible task of getting them on his feet was completed, he usually pulled them off and hunted in his usual barefooted manner.

The numbers of scents encountered, the myriad of trails crossed and followed, the thousands of retrieves, both real and practice now blur in chaotic confusion. Sometimes as a professional plant grower, I look ahead at a season before me and all that needs to be done and accomplished and am overwhelmed. I see the numbers of plants that need to be grown and delivered in the short season we call the "growing season" here in Minnesota and wonder how on earth it can all get done. Only by taking it in daily increments, now laid out by a computer into print-outs of tasks to be done each twenty-four hours, can it get done. So it seems, as I look back at Roy's days as my dog, that only by looking back a season at a time does it seem possible so much could be done.

The dog year seems to correctly amplify what a dog really does in his lifetime. It all seems to happen in hyper-dog drive. I see why so many dogs seem to operate at split-second speed, wasting no time when they are out on their given job. The drug-sniffing dog running past thousands of travelers' bags in precise cuts and curves, the herding dog running and doing one-eighties in split seconds, and the guide-dogs analyzing in moments what is needed during each minute of the day to keep their human safe—all work in dog-time amplifying their lives.

Of course our hunting dogs also run at an extremely fast pace and now I realize Roy probably lived in a particularly super-amplified time. From the late nineties until the present time in 2011, we have enjoyed extremely good times in the Midwest concerning upland bird numbers. The Dakotas, Minnesota, and eastern Montana have had agreeable winters and high acreage of Conservation Reserve Program lands, or set-aside grasslands for optimum production of pheasant and sharp-tail grouse. The environment Roy lived and hunted in offered some of the best opportunities for his occupation that we have seen in many years. He lived in what many will remember as "the good old days" of bird hunting. I suspect there are in reality many sets of "good old days" and maybe all of us and our dogs experience them.

Those of us who have been attached to hunting dogs during those years can rejoice in the fact that our canine companions had the greatest fulfillment possible for their instincts and drives. Perhaps in his twelve or so years, he really had the numbers of eighty-some years. Perhaps his joys of the hunt were truly seven-fold. Again I must ask what is time to a dog?

It seems there is no middle ground with a dog. They seem either asleep, deep in rest, or otherwise one hundred percent turned on. There is no rheostat that gradually amps a dog up as the need is felt or gradually tempers his enthusiasm to lower levels. Sometimes in the deep fall of the year we too, become them. I can see it now, looking at the shiny yellow dog in October. It was warmish, maybe sixty degrees

Roosters were Roy's greatest joy.

in the golden sun. The morning was high-strung with tall, tight cover, and later in the morning brushy coolies piercing their bony fingers through harvested wheat fields. We had worked hard and traveled fast to pin those Montana roosters before they sprinted away.

After lunch we had lain in the sun, dog and hunter, sprawled at length, absorbing the late autumn rays. We dozed and heard the breeze in semi-sleep. Maybe we heard a rooster crow in the distance, but we're not sure if we really heard it or only dreamed it.

All of us, dog and man, dream the sunny dreams of exploding color and wing beats at an imperceptible rate. We feel and smell the day. That day was at least seven times more real to both dog and hunter. Almost indistinguishably, the sunlight slanted just a bit closer to the horizon, and we became restless again, soon going at full speed to the sunset.

The miles Roy traveled by foot, began to pale before the total miles he traveled with me. Roy traveled well and traveled far. He never questioned where we were going, always happy to be along for the ride. I don't know if he anticipated some new adventure in some far away field or if he just looked forward to some place at the end of the trail where we'd share a space and get our respective bowls of food before sleep.

Sometimes the laws cause me to wonder. As I began to take Roy to different states, most required a health certificate for the dog—proof of a recent physical exam, and of course proof that all canine shots were up to date. I wondered if they felt the dog would be driving the truck, or perhaps talking to landowners about permission to hunt. There seem to be no rules for people who travel to different states, but I guess hunting dogs, who in all probability will never even come into contact with another dog or human, are subject to regulation. Roy never minded going to see the veterinarian for his annual pre-hunt check-up—maybe he connected it to a fall ritual that portended the coming hunting season. Veterinarians have always amazed me at how they seem to be able to handle pets of all types and dispositions, and put them at ease.

I haven't stopped to calculate the mileage we traveled to different states and provinces; I can't even imagine the "dog miles" he chalked up on those trips. Fall was our time, the slow season for my business, but the working time for Roy. He became the star on some of the greatest stages in the country. These were the open fields of Minnesota, the Dakotas, Montana, Manitoba, and Saskatchewan. His co-stars were the ring-necked pheasants, sharp-tail grouse, ruffed grouse, Hungarian partridge, and the amazing and beautiful waterfowl.

We were in eastern Montana, over seven hundred miles from home, and I suppose for Roy it seemed like forty-nine hundred miles. The strong smell of sagebrush pierced my nostrils as the sun took its first bite out of the horizon. We listened on that still morning and it was much like a flock of chickens in the distance.

The tree was massive and its dead white branches spread against the bluing sky. At least a hundred sharp-tailed grouse perched in the tree and chattered in the early light. Watching with binoculars I saw them disperse into a half section of tall native grassland. The area held few pheasants but obviously the sharp-tail population was great.

We pulled into the rancher's yard, the owner of the grassland. Paint had long left the sun-bleached boards of the house. A vocal dog, mostly blue heeler, greeted us. The rancher stood up alongside a drafty outbuilding where he was fixing an old hay mower. As he walked over to our truck he tossed a colorful ball toward the dog which immediately went after it and began to push it around the yard. He pushed and followed the ball relentlessly, obsessed with catching the ball. It was the kind of whacky act that should have made it onto the Jay Leno or David Letterman shows.

Roy was sleeping in the kennel box in the back of the truck as I learned that some dogs are obsessed with things far different than my dog. Maybe Roy could have gotten interested in rolling a ball around the yard, but I was happy he had other interests.

I laughed, "He sure likes to chase that ball around."

"It's what he does," the old rancher remarked as he licked the paper on a hand-rolled smoke.

We talked weather, crops, coyotes, and dogs we had known. The rancher was most agreeable to letting us pursue sharp-tail grouse in his prairie, noting that my dog needed some entertainment too.

I suppose the truth of the matter was that Roy was just as obsessed as the blue heeler, but his obsession was pheasants. It's what he grew up with, it's the colorful ball he learned to chase. "It's what he does."

We entered the grassland knowing there were plenty of grouse to be found, believing Roy would take a liking to sharp-tails as much as pheasants. After all, a bird is a bird and to the human nose they all pretty much smelled the same. When Roy hit pheasant scent in a field he trembled with excitement and his tail twitched with anticipation. This was his "birdie" mode. It comes naturally to all bird dogs.

Today he hit a new bird scent, since it was the first time we had seriously hunted him on sharp-tails. He stopped to smell and followed the trail tentatively. Although he coursed and switched as the smells led him, and his coat undulated like a Slinky going down a set of stairs, he seemed unsure if this was something we really wanted him to follow. He stopped and looked

Sharptail grouse will do in a pinch.

back, questioning if he should pursue the new scent. Yet, in his inner dog-sense it seemed like the right thing to do. The new scent just didn't elicit the excitement of a pheasant. "Go get him," I encouraged. Soon he came upon the bird and it flushed. Upon downing the bird and yelling the magical word "fetch," Roy went to the bird. I could see that he had found it, but the usual enthusiasm for the retrieve was not quite as noticeable as with a pheasant. Reluctantly he picked the grouse up and brought it to me. I'll never forget the way he cocked his head and gingerly gave me the bird. He seemed to take special pains to touch it as little as possible. The look was "what is this?"

He agreed to hunt them, and hunted like a champ, but they just didn't excite him like pheasants. Perhaps they had less scent, or maybe the taste of the feathers was less agreeable, but he just didn't have quite the excitement that he usually had.

Yet it was all good for Roy and any outing that involved birds was better than no outing at all. To be certain, there were pheasants to be found in Montana as well, and the miles were filled with great joy for both man and dog.

When Saskatchewan skies are filled with geese and ducks, what is box time to a Labrador retriever? Does an hour spent traveling to a distant hunting location seem like seven hours or one-seventh of an hour? How far is Saskatchewan? Is it seven hundred miles or forty-nine hundred miles? Does time spent in the field seem like seven times the joy of one hour, and the travel to get there only one seventh of the actual travel time?

The sounds were the first part of the experience to reach Roy's senses when we reached the great prairie province. The pure intensity of the sounds was to be savored by both dog and human. The deafening and incessant chatter of thousands of geese rising in clouds above golden grain stubble filled our auditory sense. V's of ducks swung over marsh and field and Roy's box time ended as he leapt to the

ground and immediately raised his nose to test the sumptu-
ous scents of a new world. I think about how many times he
entered his kennel box at home and emerged later into a totally new and awesome scene, one which teased his keen
senses to a new level. Indeed the new province was a new
world to Roy, and he was ready to explore it.

Here were marshes strung together like blue pearls,
threaded with flocks of ducks. Here also were farmers who
came from their houses to greet us as we drove into the yard
to ask permission to hunt. Never before have I been given
permission to hunt even before I asked for it, yet as we got
out of the truck we had a landowner say, "If you're hunters
and you want to hunt that field, go to it." He said this as we
gazed across the road onto a field that was enveloped by perhaps ten thousand snow geese.

Marshes, waterfowl, and a Labrador
retriever—it doesn't get much better.

47

Many times in Roy's career we reached such places that were truly the places our dreams were made of. The taste of the game is long gone and sadly so is Roy. The way the sunlight caught his wet, rough coat as he brought the first snow goose of his career and handed it to me still fills my mind. I still smell his scent as it mingled with the smell of the marsh, and I hear his tentative first step into the icy water and then the leap and splash as my re-assuring fetch command sent him to the downed goose with reckless abandon.

The miles and years commingled into a last day. What is time to a twelve-year-old dog as he lay panting on the floor next to his hunting partner? Do the journeys of a lifetime wander about in dog-mind splendor and wild confusion over numbers and strings of events? Is the longest mile yet to come for him? Just as we wonder if all of a dog's life is magnified or intensified by seven or some such number, the days we spend with our dog are magnified as well. So the last day is also amplified, focused, and burned into a memory of seven-fold.

S omeone once remarked to me that they wished they could get a battery-operated hunting dog that could be taken out of the closet in the fall, filled with fresh batteries and used for a couple of months. It made me think about what dog ownership is all about.

Although we relish the fall with our hunting partner in the field with us, the vast majority of the time spent with a dog is during the off season. It would seem to be a great tragedy if the greatest part of the time spent with our dog is not enjoyable. I've come to the conclusion that a dog's total personality and demeanor is more important than their hunting ability.

Indeed Roy spent more time sleeping by our bed than he spent trailing pheasants in the field. I found he spent more time doing everything else around us than he spent hunting. The dog/human role and relationship has changed since the first domestic wolf became associated with the first ancient human.

We no longer live exclusively by hunting; it is no longer our primary life's pursuit. There are times we wish it could be, especially on those golden October days that find us under blue skies and pursuing somewhat cooperative game. Yet as I look out into below zero weather, frozen fields, devoid of game and full of the treacheries of winter, I am thankful for gas furnaces and canned beans.

Our dogs have become more domesticated, and even Roy, (tough as he might seem) as he broke ice to retrieve, and hunted into blinding snow, I still know how he hurried to get out and go to the bathroom in the winter and rushed to get back into the warm house as soon a possible.

The bottom line about hunting dogs is that they are primarily pets—house dogs that fulfill mainly the needs we have for companions and friends. Roy was always the lap dog, the spoiled baby that worked his human friends for all they were worth. Roy learned quickly that good manners in the house led to good things. He quickly learned the drill. He knew he had to sit patiently to be given a bone to chew on. He quickly learned to never get his front paws off the floor and not even think about getting on furniture.

The sun slanted into the south-facing window. It was a January Saturday. Only on the rare mid-day when the sun shone brightly, did those precious rays find their way to our living room rug. Roy's golden coat glowed like fire in the little three-by-four-foot spot of sunlight.

As the afternoon progressed and the bit of warmth moved across the living room, Roy moved every half hour or so. He was determined to stay in the warmth of the sunlight. As the illuminated patch moved and Roy was left in shadow, he shook awake, rose and stretched, front legs straight and back legs bent in the canine stretch and then moved into the bright light, circled twice and finally spun himself down to the warm patch of carpet.

Roy had learned to survive the rigors of the long winter, and I had learned the simple entertainment of watching a dog sleep in the sunlight. Many times, with binoculars trained upon red fox sleeping on a snow drift in the distance, I had observed the same mid-winter shuffle as the fox would struggle to stay on the part of the snowdrift that reflected the most sunlight and warmth upon its body.

Roy had the January shuffle down to a science, and showed his great canine instinct for being able to sleep in the perfect spot. Yes, the entertainment value of a dog on cold winter days was not to be under-estimated. There was the rhythmic rise and fall of his deep chest, and the periodic twitch of ears that imagined, even in winter, the presence of marauding flies.

Days of winter should be savored with a good book and a canine upon the sleepy stage of the living-room rug. When the sun lined up just right, I could warm my feet as I sat in my favorite chair, Roy the warmest foot mat imaginable. The off-season dog was still the epitome of loyalty and function.

Spring brought work and long days with even longer nights spent at the desk. Without fail, the furry mat kept my feet warm. I wondered what the greatest joy of a hunting dog really was. Even as I worked at plans and projections for my summer livelihood, my feet found solace and warmth. Best of all, the soft furry dog sent memories of the fall to my mind, and even as I worked I reminisced of fall days and glorious times of leisure and wandering.

Just as a deer head may hang upon the wall, certainly not a trophy, but a memory, a reminder of a special day in the field, so the retriever's warmth brought memories and joy to a busy time.

As we live with our dogs, it is seldom recalled that Man and Canine were once the fiercest enemies. Man stalked the same game—a predator to be feared. The canines also stalked the warm-blooded quarry and so Man and Canine struggled over game and territory. Humans possessed a superior intellect and a mastery of tools and weapons, and the canines, of course, lived by their superior nose and cunning elusiveness.

At times Man would reach out and kill the canines, fighting to the death over hunting territory. Yet the canines survived and competed for the very food that Man needed.

Somewhere in the dim past a bond developed between the Man and some far distant relative of the dog. Perhaps it was a tenuous relationship, one born of utility and mutual interest. The canine became at first, Man's superior tool, his partner in the procuring of food. Yet slowly, over the centuries, the relationship evolved. At first the canine remained at the mouth of the cave or shelter, later moving into the home of the man.

Even now the relationship is curious as we welcome our dog to share our sustenance and our shelter, yet humans think nothing of pursuing the red fox or putting a bullet into a marauding coyote. In fact some of our dogs are actually bred and trained to hunt and pursue coyotes, long lost shirt-tail relatives now on opposite sides of the table.

I am fascinated at how some branches of the canine clan have embraced Man to be called his best friend, while others of the canine bunch still compete and pillage the things which humans call their own. Coyotes still kill sheep and calves, wolves forage upon the same moose and deer population that sportsmen also claim as their right.

At times, as Roy rested upon our floor, and he seemed in deepest reverie—sleep engulfing his total being, I saw in the slits of his eyes the deep and repressed wildness that seemed to dwell in the canine heart. So too, we humans in our dreams and deepest fantasies savor the hunt of our long passed ancestors. The most basic of common ground lies deep within both Man and dog and perhaps it howls within us at some level that eludes our consciousness.

Happily we've learned to work together, and it seems we find more, rather than less, things that we can cooperate upon. The relationships between epileptic children and their dogs (the dog having an ability to predict a seizure) is amazing. Of course it seems that companion dogs are trained to do more things for their human friends than ever before. The bond grows deeper just as our relationship with Roy grew and he became a fixture in our household. He was always the first to greet our children as they visited and the first to be acknowledged when they came.

Maybe it's the great ability of dogs to embrace routine, that endears them to humans. Their ability to get into sync with our schedules is particularly attractive to us. A canine is normally a nocturnal or a diurnal creature. Wolves and coyotes tend to hunt at night or at least in the low-light periods. Yet our dogs soon adapt to sleeping at night and being active during the day, just like people.

Roy, just like most pups, whined during his first nights with us, but soon learned to sleep at night and spend more active time during the day. He learned to hunt during the day, and to eat on a morning and evening schedule, probably quite different from the wild canine schedule.

He learned to get up in the morning, eat and go potty on a human schedule. As he grew older, the transition to human schedules seemed more and more seamless and he seemed less and less a creature to be cared for. He pretty much ate, slept, and went outside on our schedule. He got to the point of not really even needing to go to the door when he needed to go out. I suppose we really were the ones who got trained and we just instinctively knew when he needed some kind of attention.

The dog seemed to be endlessly on our periphery, always there, but never really needing much but the basics. He got to be a habit, a bit of warmth and routine that we not only grew accustomed to, but needed, to fully complete our day.

My guess is that most hunters who have dogs would never opt for a battery-operated dog, used only in the fall and then stored for the rest of the year. In fact, I'd bet that if most hunters had the option of being able to utilize their best hunting dog only for the hunting season, and then being able to save him in some sort of dormant state, they'd still opt to have him around during the off season.

If I could have just hunted Roy for the three-month season of each of his twelve years and then saved him for the nine months of the off season, it would have meant I would've been able to hunt him for four times the seasons I actually had him. Yet, there is no way I would have spent the off season without having him around.

When a dog is not around, the bare spot, the void, is strikingly evident. Even our greatest dog, our golden boy, could not be put on the shelf. They are so much more than hunting companions. Maybe it's just the constant reminder of the golden days of fall that give them such prominence in our lives, but it really is more than that. For us, as with the dogs, it goes back to the dim and distant past. For not only did that first canine come into the circle of Man's fire, but I believe he was invited to fill some great void in the soul of the man. The first scrap of meat thrown to the wolf was not an offering of truce, but a gift of friendship, an invitation to fill a deep need in the man.

Roy's last days with us were not about the hunt. They had nothing to do with his ability, or of keeping his side of the bargain. Even as he lay there on my rug during those last days, he emanated warmth and a fulfillment. Still his fur warmed my feet and I suppose my feet kept him focused.

The time now was a time that neither hunter nor dog could experience alone. The ancient canine either killed and survived or weakened and perished, and ancient Man either utilized his canine or moved on beyond the companion. It is not so easy to move beyond a friend.

I suppose the canine/human relationship has evolved over the eons of time to a type of relationship that is less utilitarian and more emotional. There is probably much to suggest that the emotional part of the dog/man bond is primarily dependent upon the emotion of Man. Yet, I knew in those waning days that Roy needed the closeness and the comfort of his human friends.

Even as he had followed me for all those years, perhaps out of habit or training, I now sensed his need to never let me get far from him. As difficult as it was to have his infected limbs bleeding upon my carpet, it was more difficult to push him away; the need was felt by both of us. Now the sense of knowing his primary function was not that of a hunting dog, trained to perform and assist, but it was a more ancient bond: the solid figure upon my front step, the protective figure of a best friend lying at the mouth of my cave.

G rowing up, Roy lived with us in a fairly busy neighborhood. It was somewhat rural, yet cars frequented our road and neighbors sprang up near us. Roy's territory seemed to encompass our home and our immediate yard. A person walking past on the road might illicit a low growl from the dog, but it was only a perfunctory admonition to beware. Someone actually entering our yard drew a more fierce response from Roy—his hackles stood up and he really seemed worried.

A dog's "red zone" seems to change with different levels of human population. As Roy got older, I began to spend more and more time at our more remote farm site. The place is located on a little-traveled gravel road with no close neighbors. We basically live there on over one hundred acres, and see few visitors besides family. Roy's tolerance for visitors became much lower at this location. How dare a car go past on our gravel road? Roy would bark whenever that happened. Pity the fool that dared to actually turn into our driveway.

I don't know why some dogs seem to fixate upon a particular person and decide to be their sole protector. Roy was that kind of dog. He didn't want to share me with anyone else. He really didn't like it when someone came between me and him. Whether he was lying on the rug by the door, or on the deck during the summer, he was the self-appointed greeter or screener of all who approached his pack-mates. Sleeping by our bed ready to defend at any moment's notice was his assumed job. Any out of place noises drew an instant reaction from Roy.

I remember having a furnace in the greenhouse not far from our house that lit very noisily during the night making a muffled sound of exploding natural gas. Roy barked and growled every time it lit and of course woke us up on those cold nights.

As Roy reached nine years old it happened that an acquaintance informed me of a litter of pups from great parents. I wasn't sure if we wanted a second dog, but stars seemed to align as they sometimes do, and one day a little chocolate Lab pup arrived on the scene. It's kind of like when you have a second child. You still want to give the older child a lot of attention, but the younger one needs a lot more attention. The young pup went through the usual puppy phases and demanded a lot of time. Roy was a bit jealous and had no time for the pup. He just needed to stay out of Roy's way or suffer a quick nip and growl.

At first Roy seemed only passively interested in the little ball of fur. After all, how long could we possibly put up with the little know-nothing pup? The pup wasn't even close to being the alpha dog in the household. Roy saw to it that the pup stayed off his designated rug and certainly never even set foot into the bedroom, which Roy co-owned with Muriel and me.

The pup trained well, all of which is another story, but his disposition was not dependent upon any one else in the household. The pup did what was expected; basically he was a "utility dog." He learned to fill in when needed. He did as much as we needed him to do. As a hunting dog he performed as expected. If Roy needed a bit of box time, the pup took up the slack.

Roy, of course, howled his discontent when the pup got to hunt. We couldn't hunt them together or the pup would have had little success. Roy always dominated, always got the work. I was always amazed that even as the younger dog became physically more adept than Roy, he never competed

Hunting Coach

with Roy. I suppose it does a person good to see that youth and stamina aren't the only things that prevail—seniority and sensibility actually count for more.

Roy had learned to hunt smart and live smart. He knew the short cuts to the quarry in the field. He knew the cover to ignore and the places to concentrate his efforts. Even though the younger dog could power through more cover and held his stamina longer, Roy still got the job done more efficiently.

It is only when you see the comparisons that you really realize the superiority. Certainly the pup was all that was advertised, but Roy was the golden boy, the genius from the other side of the tracks. But more than performance in the field was the way he lay at my feet at night, the way he still followed me. The fulfillment to his day was no longer the retrieve or the flush, but the evening on the rug snuggled close and warm to my feet. The "utility dog" did his job and was perfectly content to sleep by the door or in the basement.

The chew toys came out at night. The utility dog had at least twenty pounds on Roy but as the bones hit the floor he sat back as Roy (in leisurely fashion) selected the bone he wanted. Only after he went over to his favorite spot by the couch did the pup pick up the other bone and find a place to chew.

Roy commanded the respect of royalty. There was never any dispute about who was alpha dog. If Roy tired of the chew toy he had, he simply went over to the younger dog, who would immediately drop his bone and allow Roy to take it. Any attempt to enter our bedroom at night by the utility dog met with absolute defense by Roy. After all, our room was his adopted box and no one violated that either.

Roy settled into a zone of bonding with the people in his life, he was one of us and the pup merely was hanging around. The pup seemed only to wait for an assignment to be carried out. He needed work and thrived on it but never needed much for accolades from his human companions. Roy was only made complete by his human associations.

Before the pup arrived we needed to board Roy for a few days. We left him in good familiar hands with a person who had worked with and trained him when he was young. Roy was a total wreck, refusing to eat or even go out to exercise. He moped in his kennel and became physically sick because we weren't there for him. Of course these things made us sad but also made us feel special. On the one hand we felt badly for the dog being so lost without us but we also were secretly proud that any creature could have such devotion to us.

Amazingly, over the more than three years we had both Roy and the pup together, they bonded. Roy actually became used to the pup and even relied on him to be around.

The first time we boarded the two dogs together we were worried that if they were in the same kennel together, Roy might actually harm the pup because his frustration level with the younger dog seemed to be very high. Fortunately the people who boarded them took the effort to observe them together. Although they stayed at opposite ends of the kennel, we found that Roy appreciated the familiarity of the younger dog with him. No longer did I have to leave a t-shirt I had slept in to comfort Roy when I wasn't there.

I guess Roy finally realized the pup was a permanent fixture after about a year. He seemed to know that the utility dog had a permanent place in the household. I suppose the other good thing was that the pup learned his place in the canine pecking order. He knew to be submissive to Roy and they got along just fine. The pup would lift his chin if Roy growled—an immediate sign of submission.

Just as the unspoken rules developed between Roy and me, he learned to comply with the rules of the house without me having to constantly give him commands. The pup also learned to comply with Roy's rules. The young dog feared and respected Roy far more than he did me or Muriel. The rules became unspoken, the growls much less frequent and challenges from the pup were almost non-existent. The pup became comfortable with almost anyone who would give him an assignment. His disposition toward humans was always very sweet and agreeable. It was almost as if he assumed no responsibility for the protection of the household. He relied on Roy to take care of that duty. His role would eventually change and I noticed how his personality changed when Roy was no longer there. He has however, remained a very compliant and agreeable dog, seeming to have no protective or otherwise disagreeable traits.

We learned that even though Roy was bonded to us, and actually missed us if not there, the pup really didn't care who was around, and anyone with a cup of dog chow and a bucket of water would do just fine as a friend.

The transition during the last year that the two dogs were together was quite amazing. I was not as intrigued by any power grab by the younger dog, for he always deferred to the older dog, but rather by the way Roy began not only to accept the pup, but to allow him into his space. There were few visitors or occupants of the household who were allowed into Roy's space. To be honest we were very careful not to let crawling grand-kids toddle into Roy's designated area. We told visitors to call Roy over to them if they wanted to pet him, and with these precautions all went well.

One exception to Roy's space rule was our little grandson, who for some reason could always approach Roy and pet him, and Roy only deferred in perfect docility. Our grandson always liked Roy and for some reason they had an understanding.

Soon we began to notice that even the living-room rug became a space in which the younger dog could approach. As Roy reached ten years old, the young pup and Roy could be found sleeping on the same rug. Even in the hunting field the two would work together and for a few brief hunts the "nose up" senior and the "face to the ground" pup would quarter and cross-quarter to cover the field in perfect complement to each other. I suppose an upland bird-hunter dreams of such a perfect combination, the dream-team of hunting. It became a reality, and for a brief time I enjoyed the two dogs hunting together. Such perfect scenarios never seem to last long and so as Roy grew older, we began to hunt the two dogs separately again.

I remember vividly how he lay panting there, on a late August night in the summer of 2010, oblivious to any intrusions into his space. We came to him and his glassy eyes begged us to enter his space, to comfort and console. Spooning water into his limp and gasping mouth, I could only sit by him on the rug, only place my hand upon his head. He was oblivious then, of anything around him, unable to move. The fever and infection shot him down, mellowed those penetrating eyes to only searching orbs, crying for comfort.

It's hard to feel so needed, the burden reversed and placed upon the man, the reliance upon some human instinct now needing to be transferred to the dog.

It must be the ears, the silky smooth short fur that compels us to brush our cheek across the head of a little puppy. There in lies the essence of the dog. Maybe it's the epicenter of the dog's smell, the bonding scent you can never get out of your mind.

I am sure the scent of a dog is probably offensive to others, but the scent of your dog is the perfume of the ages. I am certain that ancient man was much more attuned to the smelling—I am sure he trusted his nose much more than we do now. Although his newly-acquired best friend of the canine genus was far more adept at the mysteries of scent, I am certain Man knew his particular dog by the scent, by the particular odor of the dog.

We get a greater appreciation of scent as we learn to know our dogs. They all smell different and we learn to know and appreciate the scent of our particular dog. Roy was the first of my indoor dogs, and with him I learned to know a dog on a much more intricate level and to become close to him. Even after a bath with dog-soap, or a retrieving plunge into a marsh, the scent still lingered, still had the same unique aroma of Roy.

Those who don't become attached to dogs will never know what I mean. To some, the dog smell is just another less-than-appealing odor. Yet we learn our dog's smell and it is a source of comfort, grounding us in the things that keep us happy. Of course, the smell of someone else's dog means little to me, yet I now know that it is important to the other person.

It's crazy, but a whiff of Roy's old collar brings back the warm thoughts of autumn days drenched in golden hues and flashing birds, or cold, dark half-frozen marshes in the deepest days of November. Such scents might cause me to put my stocking-clad feet beneath my computer desk and expect to find the soft warmth of my pup waiting. Perhaps, I'll be inspired by such a scent to look back as I walk out to my office expecting to see a little yellow pup following my footprints in the snow. It's a scent that never leaves your memory, just as surely as the scent of a person or a season or any number of smells sweeps us to a place or time to be remembered.

The dog's sense of smell is one of the great miracles of nature, but as I raised Roy I began to see for the first time how that gift can be transferred to the human as well. Of course, we will never be able to put our nose to the ground and trail a pheasant or find our way home blind-folded, only by putting our nose in the air. I did find however, that close association with your dog allows you to actually distinguish his smell from that of other dogs. Of course, it's only logical to assume that the dog can separate and distinguish the smell of every person in his life. Roy, like other dogs, knew instantly if a person was someone he knew by his smell. I suppose, I had never imagined that dogs too have their own scent.

We hear only the usual responses from people who smell dogs, like "he smells doggie," or "he smells like a wet dog." Only after you put your nose into a puppy's silky fur and inhale his scent, do you realize that it is unique, and only then will it become indelibly etched upon the hard-drive of your mind.

The strange thing is that the scent of your dog becomes a positive smell—you find it to be pleasant, soothing, and even a smell that sets you at ease. I have read studies that indicate that having a dog in the house is a positive thing from a health standpoint. I believe that just inhaling the smell of your dog brings pleasant thoughts, or perhaps in the mind of the bird-hunter, the smell of the dog puts vivid images of October, and perfect retrieves into our consciousness.

Our dogs and their scent are a perfect, live link to good times. Perhaps the scent of our dog as he lay near our head at night gives more peace and rest to our night's sleep. Maybe even the assurance he's on duty, ready to react if some terror should approach by night, gives us special comfort. Certainly I can relate to ancient man and the added peace he felt as he slept in his cave or shelter with the dog lying at the entrance, ever-vigilant.

The scent of the new pup is different. Although it too becomes a recognizable scent, it doesn't convey with it the same familiarity, the same ambiance of solidarity and harmony. Only with time, with many synchronized steps, with a great time of following, can the scent be joined to the synapses of our brain and bonded forever.

One thing is certain: even as Roy and I spent the last days together, Roy always knew my scent, always responded with his nose first. I am certain that as I put my hand on his muzzle, he took special comfort from my scent.

Even as Roy got older and I threw the retrieving dummies out, he lost touch as they went out of his sight range, but his nose always led him to the mark. As increasing symptoms began to overwhelm his other senses and voice commands began to blur and dim, he always found his way by nose. The rock solid sense of smell never let him down.

As the last day approached, he still smelled and anticipated his food. I sat down on the rug so he could lay his head on my leg and smell the comfort of a friend. The last ride in the truck was filled with the closeness of scent. He lay in the intoxicating comfort of my smell and he emanated the familiar scent of long days on the hunt and warm nights in the warmth of the evening fire.

11

L ook at the edge of his tail," she remarked, as Roy lay on the floor.

"Yeah, it looks like the hair has worn off the edge, where he wags his tail when he's lying down." He knew we were talking about him and he wagged his tail again, scratching the floor in a wide arc.

As I made supper, Roy was sprawled on the floor. The slightest look or smile from me caused that tail to wag along the floor, as if he were trying to sweep it clean. Obviously sweeping his tail over the floor or on the rug would wear the hair from the sides of his tail. We thought little of the bare edges of his tail until I took Roy to the veterinarian for a routine physical. Roy would be going to South Dakota and needed his health certificate. All was fine at that point and only a comment from the doctor, "He seems to be losing the hair on his tail," got my causal reply, "It's probably from wagging his tail when he lies on the floor."

"If he shows any signs of distress we can do some tests."

Roy seemed fine, hunted like his old self and acted normal that fall. That fall of 2009 was a busy fall, the new pup sharing the hunting spot-light, but Roy still seemed to be doing great at nearly eleven years old. He was still with me that fall, heart and soul were entrenched in the hunt, and he never let me down as we wandered through another perfect fall. Such seasons of the fall hunt seemed to string along in an endless succession and we followed each other's tracks at the appropriate times, knowing with little verbal communication what we each needed to do.

An employee commented that winter, "Old Roy still looks good," as the dog followed me out to the greenhouse. Despite the slow baring of his tail and the hint of glassiness in his eyes, he was alert and mostly himself.

"Old Roy seems to be getting a bit of a pot belly, probably lying around too much during the winter," someone else mentioned.

"Maybe I need to cut his feed a bit during the off-season," I replied. Yet Roy seemed more hungry than ever and I couldn't find it in my heart to cut down on his feed.

The busy spring embraced us, led us from busy day to busy day. Each night he lay sprawled by my bedside, exhausted from watching me run double-time all day.

I knew in my heart that the panting was not his usual self. He stretched with his tongue extended, his chest heaving in double-time. Yet, the cooling evening would spread upon the floor and Roy would settle to his night's sleep.

It was during the busy May season I knew he needed to be checked by the veterinarian.

"We should do a thyroid check," she assessed.

The abnormality demanded thyrozine to correct thyroid deficiency. The re-check in June showed improvement and Roy seemed to be doing okay. He was maybe a little slower, but still very much with it. I'd throw the scented retrieving dummy into the tall Bluestem grass behind the house and he gleefully hunted and retrieved it. Roy shifted to past years upon the retrieve, and the puppyish glee returned to his eyes as he fetched the fake pheasant from the tall grass.

The ball of yellow fur was the usual fixture by our supper table and next to our bed. Roy just seemed to revel in the closeness we kept. He always seemed to know exactly where he was supposed to be in our household.

"It must be the heat," she reassured me. Roy was panting as we sat on the deck. It was a warm summer, and of course dogs suffered like we all do during those hot August days. Yet it was the panting, the patterned beat, the nearly endless gasps, that told the tale. Even into the cool of the night, he'd pant. Here in Minnesota, even the hottest days can cool off into nights which are comfortable for sleeping. Even as the nights cooled, the panting of the dog was evident.

Sometime during the warm summer our trails seemed to part in at least a partial manner. Something took him away, pulled his trail to other concerns. Every trail has a fork, the place where new vistas are required. The road is never straight and eternal. New needs, new forces were beginning to engulf Roy. A new battle swept upon him.

The dog-rule of seven now reared its sometimes-ugly head. I suppose most dog owners wish that the seven-concept would work in the opposite way. They wish that for every year of the dog they could get seven real-time years. Most would perhaps endure seven years of potty-training or fourteen years of chewing carpets and dragging things around the house. Yet the rule of seven would quickly drag Roy from us, until the cold day in November, still panting and glassy-eyed, his tracks in the November snow would veer off and be covered by the prairie wind.

❖12❖

There was a time when I believed August to be a month engulfed in serenity—static and changeless. I thought it to be a month of sweet corn and warm nights for swimming, days of endless harvest. August has always painted itself as a green and full month, one that seems almost never-ending in its abundance.

Now I have come to realize it is more a month of change than I had previously thought. The Bluestem grass in the prairie takes on the subtle change of color that portends the fall flash of grandeur. The yellow and bronze of the late-summer and fall flowers begin to announce the change of the season. Even the local geese are now restless, would have their young in nervous flight, readying for a longer flight still unknown to the young of the year.

The August of 2010 was to proclaim a fall of change and it was announced to me as I woke on the eleventh of the month. The panting of course had become routine and I wasn't surprised that Roy lay breathing heavily. He seemed to be licking his left front leg. Again, not unusual for a dog that, throughout his life, had always meticulously licked and cleaned his paws and fur.

Now in the early morning light I saw the source of his attention: the left front leg being swollen to several times its normal size. The skin beneath the fur was red and a callous on the leg was oozing fluid. Roy, of course, was limping badly and was able to put no weight on the leg.

The fact that the incredibly swollen leg came over night has never ceased to amaze me. Roy ate and went outside and we felt we should see how he did. The swelling got no better and we decided to call the vet. We were able to get an appointment for the next morning and were advised to keep an eye on the leg.

Keeping an eye on it wasn't a problem, as it was an extraordinary sight. The leg seemed very tight and hard, apparently filled with some infected fluid and totally inflamed.

That night he lay on the living room floor, sprawled on his side, tongue lolling out of his mouth and panting. For the first time ever, he wouldn't get up, wouldn't respond. I knew he needed to drink, yet he didn't have the strength to turn his head to a dish of water.

I held my hand under his mouth and spooned water into his throat. At last, he was able to swallow the water! After an hour or two of spoon-feeding the water, he responded and seemed to perk up a bit.

We thought he was a goner, but Roy finally was able to get up and move to our bedside where he seemed to recover somewhat over the night.

The next day we took Roy to the veterinarian. The leg seemed very infected and she felt we should try an antibiotic to try to clear up the leg. The vet wasn't sure if the antibiotic would solve the problem or not.

We discussed a number of symptoms: the panting and thirst, the distended stomach, his increase in appetite, and of course the sudden, severe infection. We agreed to leave Roy overnight so they could dress the leg and monitor the response to the medication.

The visit to the veterinarian also brought another change—a new word for my vocabulary. She talked of Cushing's Disease and the fact that Roy had many of the symptoms. We returned home without our dog, an empty spot on the front seat.

As the day wound down to late afternoon, I instinctively felt it was time to feed Roy and go for a walk, but he wasn't there. At suppertime I looked to see him curled on the rug, but of course it was empty.

We hoped the antibiotics would help and anticipated a phone call in the morning. Roy's tracks had veered from ours, taken a detour to someone who could perhaps care for him in a way that we couldn't.

The next evening I swung my feet out of bed and had to step wide to miss the golden mound of fur on the floor. Roy was back, the antibiotics had begun to work their magic. The swelling in his leg had begun to subside and he was even able to walk on the leg again.

We had a prescription of Baytril, in the form of grotesquely large pills to be given every evening. It had become easy to administer pills to Roy. His hunger had become extremely intense and a bit of peanut-butter wrapped around any pill was swallowed in the blink of an eye. Yet I marveled at the quick response to the medicine, and how Roy recovered from the terrible infection.

By the next day we resumed our walks and he seemed even a bit more content. Perhaps we could get the sore leg healed and get him back to the old normal.

One learns to appreciate normality and old routines when they are disrupted. We had become accustomed to the regular routine of feeding him twice day, his brief trips outside to go to the bathroom, and his regular presence in our daily lives.

Despite the reprieve, I began to see other subtle changes creep into my dog's life. I began to see the extra effort needed for him to negotiate the stairs. It wasn't just the front leg but now; the rear hips began to shake and wobble as he stubbornly followed me in my daily routine. His tracks were still religiously with me, but slower, more guarded, less perky.

When Roy was two we had his hips checked, wondering if we should perhaps someday get a puppy from him. The vet said his hips were okay, but not perfect.

"They should present no problems until much later in his life," we were told. We decided not to propagate anything

69

but flawless hip genetics, and now we were realizing it was indeed later in life for Roy.

The front leg returned to its normal size and for that we were very happy. Yet, the thirst and hunger became more pronounced. Roy was drinking a pail of water every-day, probably twice what he normally drank. Roy had never been a voracious eater. He ate his food thoughtfully, as if to savor it in some elegant way. Now he began to gobble his food voraciously. No one dared to come between him and his bowl of food.

We normally gave him a rawhide chew toy which he would chew on for days in an on-and-off fashion. Now when given a chew toy he would relentlessly chew it to bits without taking a break, completely devouring it in a short time.

Changes in his habits and attitude began to show up. New forces began to take over his life. Roy's tracks began to veer in different paths. We had come to depend upon Roy in many ways. He was the perfect dog around the house. He never dreamed of getting on the furniture and knew instinctively what things were his to touch and what was completely off limits for him. He never touched our stuff, never would even pick up an item from the floor that wasn't his. Certainly he had designated chew-toys or bones that were his, but he was totally dependable. We could leave him alone in the house if we went out, and when we returned he'd still be lying in the same place on the rug, nothing ever touched.

The path of hunger seemed to be the hardest for Roy to resist. We were taken completely off guard when Roy got into the garbage for the first time. I couldn't believe what had gotten into him. He seemed to try to pick any food-like materials he could get.

When I scolded him for his transgression, he seemed to know he had done wrong, yet I got the feeling that "the Devil made him do it."

Roy was slowly being taken over and driven by a new force, which overrode all his training and discipline. I put a lock on the garbage can and even that (with time) he was able to figure out, to the point that I had to upgrade the latching mechanism.

As fall approached, I began to realize that another area was in great jeopardy. Roy had always been the perfect retriever. He returned downed game birds to me in unscathed condition. In fact retrieving was his life. His greatest joy, it seemed, was to bring game to me. Even wounded birds were brought in un-marked by his teeth. But I began to realize that Roy could not retrieve, that his great hunger would cause him to treat any game bird as a meal to assuage his hunger. Perhaps his greatest joy as a dog was now no longer a possibility. The retrieving tracks that tied us together for so many years now had veered off to a new reality.

One day, after a successful hunt with our younger retriever, we set some pheasants on the ground in the yard. While the birds were unattended for a short time Roy snuck in, grabbed a pheasant and made a meal of it. This was so out of character for him and he seemed in another world as he devoured the bird. There was no way we were going to take that food from him!

Of course the crazy hunger caused him to eat things that were not good for him and intestinal irregularities became common. One time shortly after I mowed the lawn, Roy went outside to go to the bathroom and began to eat chunks of grass-clippings. It reached the point that he had to be monitored constantly, or the consequences to him and to our carpet would be severe.

By mid-October Roy was ingesting some pretty gross materials. Roy learned to locate and dig potatoes from the garden, along with radishes and even chunks of manure that had been tilled into the soil. He became very ill with diarrhea. We put him on a special diet of canned food and a prescription to alleviate the diarrhea. It became very difficult to keep him on the thyroid medication. The accidents when he had diarrhea were very difficult. Of course for a dog so well house trained, it was evident he also was much bothered by not making it outside.

The diarrhea finally seemed to be under control and with stringent monitoring and a regulated diet we seemed to have it under control. Our veterinarian searched for a solution to the apparent symptoms of the Cushing's Disease. She had worked in the past with an herbal homeopathic product that had shown great promise for Cushing's. We began to give Roy Uro-G Plus. Four pills twice daily was the initial dose, and he just ate them from my hand. No disguise was needed to get him to swallow the pills.

We began to see some improvement—he became less restless, slept with less panting and stress. The hunger seemed less severe, the water consumption and panting throughout the night abated. It seemed that his tracks again merged with ours. The old familiar yellow dog lay near our bed, content and restful.

The old dog of past hunts seemed to re-emerge. I threw scented retrieving dummies into the tall, golden grass of late October and Roy, ever alert, hunted them from the dense cover and retrieved them to my hand. I squinted into the ever-lowering fall sun and saw only a golden blur of fur bouncing between the fall-bronzed clumps of Bluestem grass. It was a vision of old times—his enthusiastic retrieves executed with youth and intensity. He was a working dog and only when working for me in his innate field was he truly fulfilled.

"One more time old boy," I said as I loaded my shotgun. It was a warm day for late October, the sun blessed us, and when I brought out the shotgun his demeanor lit up to the look of falls past.

We headed out into the familiar field behind the house. These were our favorite haunts—the mix of prairie grass, bounded by harvested grain fields, laced with willow draws. Roy knew theses patches of cover. I wondered how many times we had searched these coverts for elusive ring-necked pheasants.

Either by shear instinct or by memory, Roy knew how to work these patches of upland cover. To be certain he had slowed, but despite slowed reflexes and less than optimum strength, Roy's nose had not let him down.

I still remember the vivid details of that day. It was a day of primitive perfection—one man and one dog joined as the partners some ancient bond had instituted. His black nose quivered in excited and heightened intensity. As the sun hit his coat and the breeze rippled his silky ears, he looked as though he had been painted in perfection by some great artist. The day melted all signs of age and imperfection. In his eyes, so often of late dimmed in misery and doubt, I saw the old spark of enthusiasm and intensity. I watched his tail as he worked his nose up into the wind, and at times down into the cover. I don't recall the worn and hairless edges of his wagging tail on that day in the sun. The tail would tell me what his nose was detecting. As he hit the scent of birds, his body tightened and his tail became a supersonic indicator of birds near. The smell of birds drove Roy beyond the less-than-optimum physical ability he now possessed.

It was a day of dog-dreams intensified to seven times their usual strength. Dog-dreams are all that really matter on those perfect days in late October, when a hunter is following a good dog. I followed his lead, pursued his tracks, as he, for a brief moment, took the lead, telling me what was important, what mattered on that fall day. Sometimes the heavens open, granting a fore-taste of bliss, just as ancient prophets wrote of visions. Perhaps such visions are granted to dogs and hunters on late October days.

❖13❖

November is the cloudiest month of the year in Minnesota. The November of 2010 brought no surprises, treated us to no special days of warmth and sun. November is truly the month of decisive transition. September and October may hint at colder, shorter days, but they always seem to grant a reprieve. Even late October can caress us with warmth and beauty, but November is the real deal, it shows no particular mercy. There's no messing around in November—when it sets its mind to bringing clouds, cold, and frozen precipitation, it's for real. Snow that falls in November, has an honest shot at still being around in April.

The golden days of late October, turned to gray quickly in 2010, as November caused us to cherish even more, the few dazzling days of amnesty. Certainly, even in November there can be days of fallish beauty. The November of 2010 was to grant us none of those favors. It became a downward slide that could only land us in December and finally bottom out in January and February.

The first week of November it returned. The restless panting was back, and worst of all the insidious infection in Roy's left front leg. The leg was swollen again as we woke to the panting and licking sounds. The callous on his elbow had popped open and puss and blood now oozed from the wound.

I immediately made an appointment for Roy to be seen by the veterinarian. She taught me to wrap and bandage the wound, and to bind the swollen leg firmly. Roy was also put on antibiotics again along with the herbal pills and the thyroid pills. It seemed like Roy's meal time was more medication than food. He just ate the meds up like food, as his hunger seemed to drive him to eat anything he could.

Each day I changed his bandages. I looked into the gaping hole in his leg and hoped each time to see some sign of healing or perhaps a lessening of the swelling. The miracle of the antibiotics that seemed to occur the first time the infection hit him seemed not to be on the docket this time.

Now it was again the time of tracks. Snow lay on the ground. I suppose those of us who live in the northern areas become more cognizant of tracks. A good portion of the year, our landscape is covered in snow and tracks are a brazen fact of life.

Indeed, tracks are certainly apparent in mud and dust and even on tropical beaches, but snow is still the greatest reflection of recent activity. Snow shows us the most recent history, the newest events of each day. Snow can cover the past, leave buried the tall golden grass, covering it for the winter. Tracks in the frozen mud are covered until spring. Snow can bring an end to a season. Yet snow tells the innocent story of all that comes to pass in the frozen time. Snow came in November, and Roy's tracks dented the first inches as he struggled down the stairs each day to meet the whiteness and add his marks to the hoary covering.

Snow can hide nothing that takes place upon its surface, for it is the revealer of every detail. It leads the hunter to the kill. It shows the red-marked signs of every predation. So Roy's tracks marked our yard, sometimes his blood was a stark contrast to the perfect whiteness. The tracks were aimless now, splayed and uncertain, not the tracks of the disciplined hunter, or the impassioned follower. Roy's tracks now veered off in a way that tore him from our grasp.

Tracks in the snow can teach us much, and at times leave us with more questions than they answer. I wonder at the bird tracks that disappear with light wing-marks at their side. Was the bird frightened into flight, or was some primal call, some basic instinct such as food or shelter the motivation for flight? When I see a set of mink tracks disappear into a hole near a lake, I wonder if the little predator has fed and seeks shelter or if his hunger has led him to seek the possibility of a meal in the burrow he enters.

In those November days I puzzled at Roy's tracks, not the loyal tracks of the follower, nor the tracks of the confident leader, but a new set of tracks focused on some new endeavor I couldn't know. The daily marks found their way in and out of our door with increased difficulty. The tracks inside the house now were marked by blood.

I woke one morning to a pool of blood on the bedroom carpet, for Roy had pulled his bandage off and bled from his wound. The struggle began, as I tried to keep the bandages on his leg. He had been submissive to my daily bandaging of his wounds for a week and a half, but now he seemed to tolerate no more of it. Each time I carefully bound his swollen and un-healing leg, he tore the bandage free and insisted upon freeing the leg from its shackles.

Each time he tore the white strips from his leg he looked at me with glassy eyes as though I should do better, promising to tear them away again if I couldn't initiate some kind of remedy beyond a simple cover-up.

The tracks wavered, splayed off to new tangents, places we'd never explored. The snow wasn't deep, yet he struggled much as that first day that he followed my deep tracks in fresh February snow.

The tracks would lead to an old friend—the truck he so loved to ride. Certainly not the truck of years gone by he had so often leapt into. Perhaps the second or third or maybe even the fourth truck. All were his greatest joy to board and ride, allowing the tracks to be made with no effort on his part.

We approached slowly, for most things now went slowly for Roy. I opened the door and he raised his head, looking in longingly at the front seat.

"You want to ride in the truck?" The question was met with a slow wag of a now nearly hairless tail. I scooped him up in my arms, now seeming lighter and more frail than I ever could remember him, completely submissive. He leaned against the seat as I got in beside him, finally lying down next to me. As I began to drive he edged over and put his head on my leg. My hand found its usual spot on his soft head as I drove.

The sky spit little balls of snow and the road was covered in compacted snow. We drove the familiar gravel road, a road Roy knew by memory for its bumps and turns. Struggling to sit up he just had to have a look out at the grassy ditches, perhaps still hoping to catch a glimpse of an old long-tailed rooster pheasant trying to conjure his own survival plan for the now-impending winter.

Roy took a brief view of the fields. These were his haunts, his places of pleasant work. These were the marshes and meadows that were crisscrossed with his tracks and now as his final tracks crossed them, he was drawn away. Now his tracks would angle away, wander off into the north wind and be drifted over forever.

Gene R. Stark

Roy